First Printing
April 2023

THE POISON TULIP

Additional copies can be obtained from:

Disciple Maker Ministries
905 Golf Course Rd. N.W.
Hutchinson, MN 55350

612-750-5515

LanceKetchum@msn.com
www.disciplemakerministries.org

ISBN: 979-8-9877195-5-8

IN APPRECIATION

A special THANK YOU to the members and friends of Shepherd's Fold Baptist Church of Hutchinson, Minnesota for their patience with me in the unfolding and development of the truths contained in this book. You have helped me to grow through these studies. God blessed in the many decisions that you made to the glory of God during the preaching of this series. It has also been a blessing to see the increase of spiritual fruit through your lives as you began to implement the doctrine of Grace into the practice of your everyday lives. Praise God for many of you who have come to receive the gift of God's salvation through the preaching and teaching of the truths of God's wondrous Gospel.

I also want to thank Mrs. Julie Rydberg for her careful and meticulous proofreading of the manuscript. I pray our Lord will bless you in a special way for your generosity in giving many hours to this work.

To my wife, Patty – thank you for your patience in allowing me every free moment of our lives together for the last year to finish this work. You catered to my every need to allow me the time I needed. Your graciousness has exemplified all the truths defined by the doctrine of Grace. Your self-sacrificing love reveals the selflessness that manifests the Spirit-filled life. You are undoubtedly a living definition exemplifying the word "helpmeet."

Index

Bibliography
Page 163

The Poisoned Tulip
The Corporate/Vocational View of Election
Introduction

Theology is defined as the study of the attributes, nature, character, and will of God. However, there are numerous approaches to this study. For the Bible believer, the sole source of knowledge about God is *Sola Scriptura* (the Bible alone). There are many who claim to be *Sola Scriptura*, but who integrate philosophical arguments into their theology. Others are Pluralists and integrate pagan ideas of pagan gods and pagan writings into their theology.

One of these philosophical ideas about God that was integrated into Christianity from the pagan culture was the idea called *Fatalism* or *Predeterminism*. Although almost every Calvinist will deny it, *Fatalism* is very much the foundation of Calvinism's *Sovereign Grace* philosophy. Augustine of Hippo (354-430 A.D.) is credited with integrating the Greek Aristotelian philosophy of *Fatalism* into Christian theology creating a *theological Fatalism*, which developed into the *Sovereign Grace* teachings of Calvinism. *Sovereign Grace* teaching is *philosophical Fatalism*. ***Sovereign Grace* teaching is not Biblical. *Sovereign* Grace teaching is what poisons the TULIP.** Sovereign Grace teaching greatly distorts the attributes, nature, character, and will of God.

"[14] Of these things put *them* in remembrance, charging *them* before the Lord that they strive not about words to no profit, *but* to the subverting of the hearers. [15] Study to shew thyself approved unto God, a workman that needeth not to be ashamed, **rightly dividing the word of truth**. [16] But shun profane *and* vain babblings: for they will increase unto more ungodliness. [17] And their word will eat as doth a canker: of whom is Hymenaeus and Philetus; [18] Who concerning the truth have erred, saying that the resurrection is past already; and overthrow the faith of some" (II Timothy 2:14-18).

The theological term for "rightly dividing the word of truth" is Hermeneutics. TULIP theology is not based on Hermeneutics. TULIP theology is *eisegetical* (read into the Scriptures), not *exegetical* {coming out of the Scriptures).

The TULIP acronym does not actually come from Calvin or Augustine. The TULIP acronym comes from the Dutch Reformed church and the Synod of Dort (1618–1619) led by Theodore Beza and other Calvinists. The Synod of Dort listed what came to be called "the five heads of Dort" in the acronym TULIP. **Sadly, not one single letter of this acronym is Biblically accurate theology as they defined them.**

Total Depravity
Unconditional Election
Limited Atonement
Irresistible Grace
Perseverance of the Saints (*the Elect*)

***Sovereign Grace* teaching (Fatalism, Determinism, Predestination) then *presupposes* itself upon the Biblical word *election*.** In *Sovereign Grace* teaching, God *pretemporally* (before time), *unconditionally* chose all those in time that would be saved from the curse. Since these fallen beings would be "dead in trespasses and sins" and dead men cannot do anything, it would be necessary for God to **regenerate them before they could be saved.** In this regeneration, God would give them the gifts of the Holy Spirit, faith, and repentance. **The word Calvinists use to describe *regeneration before salvation* is the word *Monergism*.** Then, eventually these regenerated *elects* will not be able to resist the drawing of God's *Sovereign Grace* and they will repent and place faith in Christ. None of this has any foundation in Scripture. All of this is presupposed and imposed upon select Bible texts to make these texts say what the Calvinists want them to say. **The word election in the Bible is NEVER used in the context of God choosing someone to be saved - not even once!**

The other side of pretemporal (before time) election through God's Sovereign Grace is *pretemporal condemnation* **(reprobation).** This simply means that only those that God has *chosen* can be saved. God will not draw those He has not chosen to be saved. All the *non-elect* are hopelessly lost for all eternity. This is a radical departure from the loving God of the Bible who wants to see all come to repentance and the understanding of the Gospel of Jesus Christ.

In the day and age of *milk and cookies theology,* **there is seldom much hunger for the** *meat* **of God's Word. However, true theology is a** *line upon line, precept upon precept work.* This detailed research is not for the *milk and cookies* crowd. "Rightly dividing the Word of Truth" requires careful and meticulous examination of the Biblical data of all that God has said about a topic from cover to cover, and in minute detail (*inductive methodology*). However, in this detailed research of what God has said, we must approach with caution lest we interject or impose our own ideas or philosophies upon what God has said (*presuppositionalism*). Thereby, we would misrepresent what God has said.

The discussions surrounding Calvinism, Arminianism, Covenant Theology, and Reformed Theology has been going on for centuries. This discussion undoubtedly has been a heated discussion involving numerous points of view. This discussion involves even more numerous positions resulting in hundreds of variations and degrees of disagreement. These hundreds of variations have resulted in many, many articles, and many books. However, in most cases, these are philosophical arguments, not Biblical arguments, that are based upon solid Biblical exegesis.

If a faulty hermeneutic is used, there is little possibility of discovering what God has said and "rightly dividing the word of truth." In most of the things written on these issues and in most of the discussions about these issues, there is a blending and merging of philosophy and Bible in varying degrees. Obviously, intelligent people are trying to reconcile the incoherency of the things they read or hear regarding these discussions. **Philosophical presuppositions are hindrances, not helps.**

Perhaps the problem really lies in trying to reconcile irreconcilable doctrinal statements. Perhaps they are irreconcilable because they really are not Scriptural in the first place. The honest theologian involved in the science of Hermeneutics will honestly consider this possibility and begin to look for answers to irreconcilable issues outside of the dynamic of these ongoing theological debates. If we are going to find the answer to these issues, those answers will be found in *Sola Scriptura*. **God is not the author of confusion.**

The issues of Calvinism, Arminianism, and Covenant/Reformed Theology has been a source of great frustration for many Bible students over the history of the Church Age. The struggle of those trying to reform Roman Catholic doctrine was trying to reconcile irreconcilable statements and beliefs with Scripture. This happens because those positions have no basis in Scripture in the first place. Many have struggled with finding God's answers to these issues. The greatest frustration for most people was seeing men that are loved and respected adopt methodologies of

Biblical interpretation that were so obviously faulty. It was the use of these faulty methodologies that led them to the systems of theology they now embrace. **It seemed obvious that once they had been trained in a certain hermeneutical methodology with accompanying deductive presuppositions, that the outcomes of a theological position can be predetermined.**

The greatest frustration is seeing hundreds of young men who desire proper training to study and communicate God's truths being trained in institutions that use these faulty methodologies (*presuppositionalism*). These young men attend Bible colleges and seminaries trusting that the teachers know what they are doing and that these men are authorities in the academic areas in which they teach, especially in Biblical hermeneutics.

Surely many men professing to be Calvinists are men of God who genuinely love the Lord Jesus and seek to serve Him the best they can. There are good men who are on all sides of these issues. There are people who have invested thousands upon thousands of hours searching the Scriptures for answers to these issues. These men will not be easily convinced that the positions they hold are contrary to what God teaches in His Word. Dogmatists are dogmatists because they have diligently researched their positions and believe those positions to be *anchored to the Rock.* They should be respected for their efforts, but that does not mean false theology should be tolerated (Psalm 119:104).

I certainly do not hold myself up as the standard of Biblical orthodoxy. I say this lest I be accused of arrogance. However, I do ask that the thousands upon thousands of hours I have invested in the study of these issues at least be considered by those truly seeking truth, for that is all that I am attempting to present in these studies, i.e., what I believe God's Word says. I do not seek fame, and I certainly have no hope of fortune. I simply want to see God glorified by accurately revealing Who He is according to the revelation of His inspired Scriptures.

I have discussed and debated these issues with hundreds of men. I have been involved with panel discussions of these issues with some of the finest theological minds in modern day fundamentalism. I have read every book written on these issues that I could get my hands on. I have read Augustine. I have read Calvin. I have read Luther. I have read Zwingli. I have read and studied the Dutch Remonstrance of 1610, the Cannons of Dort, the Westminster Confession, the London Baptist Confessions of 1644 and 1689. I have read almost every published work on these issues in the last twenty-five years. I have traveled across this country from shore to shore to hear the best minds of our day debate these issues. I know many of these men personally. I say all this lest I be accused of ignorance. Granted, some may still question my conclusions, but please do not accuse me of ignorance.

What the Scriptures say will be the occupation of these studies. I will not be giving copious amounts of space or spending a great deal of time arguing with men who have been dead for five-hundred years (or more). I may refer to them occasionally and to what they have said, but I will be preoccupied with what God has said in His Word. These studies will focus on being *Sola Scriptura*. In other words, I will not be preoccupied with merely proclaiming a statement of faith in *Sola Scriptura*. I will do all I can to present a position which is truly *Sola Scriptura*.

Almost everyone I know holding to contradicting positions on these issues will make the same claim, but I respectfully state that when presuppositions are imposed upon Scripture interpretation, that these presuppositions immediately reduce true Biblical *exegesis* to *eisegesis* and a resulting faulty theology when those presuppositions are often unbiblical and/or extra-biblical. These presuppositions may by chance be proven

Biblical, but this a dangerous methodology resulting in looking for and positing *proof texts* to support the presuppositions. This has been my experience in debate and discussion with most Calvinists, Arminians, and Covenant Theologians. They quote a Bible text on which they have imposed their presuppositions and then require an explanation according to those presuppositions, never even considering their presuppositions may be wrong. They just cannot understand why others cannot see what is so obvious to them. Of course, the reason others do not see what is so obvious to them is that these others are not looking at the text through the *lenses* of their presuppositions.

Although we will look at this later, in Calvin's preface to his **Institutes of the Christian Religion** (second edition of 1539), we find a defining statement that explains to us why the *exegesis* of all Calvinists is perverted, transforming it into *eisegesis.* This happens because all Calvinists look at the Scriptures through the *theological presuppositions* of Calvin. **Calvin's *purpose* in writing his Institutes of the Christian Religion is to engrain these presuppositions into the minds of the readers of the Bible. Calvin clearly states this in his preface.**

"I have endeavored to give such a summary of religion in all its parts (*in the Systematic Theology laid out in his Institutes of the Christian Religion*), and have digested it into such an order as may make it not difficult for anyone who is rightly acquainted with it (*the Systematic Theology laid out in his Institutes of the Christian Religion*) to ascertain both what he ought principally **to look for** in Scripture, and also to what head he ought to refer whatever is contained in it. **Having thus, as it were, paved the way**, I shall not feel it necessary in any Commentaries on Scripture which I may afterwards publish to enter long discussions of doctrine or dilate on commonplaces, and will therefore always compress them. In this way the pious reader will be saved much trouble and weariness, **provided he comes furnished with a knowledge of the present work** (*the Systematic Theology laid out in his Institutes of the Christian Religion*) as an **essential prerequisite.**[1] (Bolding and parenthesized areas added.)

There were two basic theological positions of *Sola Scriptura* coming out of the Reformation. One basically said, *whatever the Bible does not disallow, we allow.* The other basically said, *whatever the Bible confirms, we confirm.* Neither position was immune from the imposition of presuppositions and proof-texting. Those coming out of Roman Catholicism (the Reformers) were especially prone to two other faulty methodologies: the *imposition of presuppositions* and *proof-texting.*

Most of the Reformers were trained theologians. However, we fail to consider that they were very *poorly trained* theologians, especially in hermeneutics. Many will find this statement offensive. However, considering the Ecclesiology, Soteriology, Pneumatology, and Eschatology of most of these men, we must conclude that the statement is true. These men came to the Bible with presuppositions that were almost totally wrong. They, in fact, simply began looking for textual *proofs* for those beliefs. For what they could not find *proof texts*, they disallowed or rejected. In other words, they came to the Bible with hundreds of presuppositions looking for Biblical support (*proof texts*) for those presuppositions. This *proof text* methodology has been the basis for Roman Catholic and

---

[1] As quoted by Robert Shank, **Elect in the Son**, A Study of the Doctrine of Election, Bethany House Publishers, Minneapolis, MN, 1970, pages 227-228

Covenant/Reformed arguments about baptismal regeneration and *paedobaptism* for centuries.

Therefore, their presuppositions must be taught *before* they ask you to begin looking at their *proof texts*. This is what is still going on in varying degrees in many of our fundamental Bible colleges and seminaries today. We must remember that almost every Reformer continued to hold to and propagate the major errors of Augustine's original Covenant Theology[2].

The Reformers continued to teach that the nation of Israel was *cast away* by God and replaced with the Theonomic institution called "the church" resulting in various state churches in various countries around the world. They continued to teach that circumcision was replaced by infant baptism. They continued to propagate sacerdotalism and the conferring of grace through sacerdotalism and sacramentalism. Although many claimed to teach justification by grace through faith, that faith was still in the *system*, i.e., the conference of grace to the participant in the sacrament through the hands of a clergyman ordained by the *church*. We must admit that their understanding of salvation —by grace through faith was radically different than what true (not *new*) Evangelicalism had held through the centuries. Even for the Evangelical Calvinist today, being saved *by grace through faith* is really defined by their doctrine of Monergism (regeneration by God preceding a decision of faith).

Interspersed into all of this was the influence and integration of various pagan philosophies and

---

[2] Yes, I am aware that Kaspar Olevianus (1536-1587) is credited with systematizing Covenant Theology according to Louis Berkhof (quoted in There Really Is a Difference by Renald E. Showers published by The Friends of Israel Gospel Ministry, Inc., page 7). However, we must credit Augustine and his Preterism with some of the original ideas that became the foundations for Covenant Theology.

philosophical methodologies. We find the influence of the philosophies of early Christian Gnosticism (manifested in the Calvinistic term *secret gospel* and *saving knowledge*), Plato, Aristotle, Socrates, and Pliny upon the thinking of the Reformers (what we know as a *classical theological* education). Many of the ideas of these pagan philosophers were the basis for theological methodologies based in *logic.* Many of their presuppositions were then imposed upon the Scriptures throughout the ages in varying degrees.

Aristotelian Syllogism (deductive logic as a methodology to deduce truth) may **have been one of the most accepted methods that resulted in many false theological positions.** This methodology was certainly a major influence upon Augustine. (*Calvinism is really nothing more than a restatement of Augustinianism.*)

Therefore, it can be said unequivocally that Augustinianism and Calvinism are *logical* systems of theology. It can also be said unequivocally that *Aristotelian Syllogism* is a faulty methodology for a solidly *Sola Scriptura* theology. If no one else, Augustine has proven that *Aristotelian Syllogism* is a faulty methodology all by himself. He can be credited with introducing more heresy into Christianity than almost any man in history. It can be said that Augustine is the progenitor of Roman Catholic Systematic Theology and should be credited with the original ideas surrounding the confusion of God's covenants upon which Covenant Theology was systematized.

Reformed Theology is the *reformed* or *corrected* Augustinian Theology. The original ideas that were the foundation for Covenant Theology were originally Augustinianism or systematized Roman Catholicism. The original Augustinian Theology was corrected in three major areas of theology:

> Ecclesiology
> Eschatology
> Soteriology

The Reformation's Ecclesiological reforms involved many degrees of change. However, most Reformers continued to hold to state churches with sacerdotal systems and sacramental conferences of God's grace. This was all practiced within false hierarchal forms of church polity. The vast majority continued to hold to a Theonomic world view of the Church's purpose on earth. **Therefore, the Reformation did not change Augustine's or Roman Catholicism's view of Ecclesiology in any real ways except in rejecting Papalism and some of the sacraments.** They continued to view church membership, water baptism, and *Holy Communion* as sacramental (*means of conferring grace to participants through the hands of ordained clergymen*). The *entrance* into the *possibility* (hope) of salvation was found only through baptism into whatever state church a Reformer viewed as correct. Reformed Theology continued to be primarily Roman Catholic (Augustinian) in their Ecclesiology.

The Reformation's Eschatological reforms hardly changed Augustine's positions at all (if at all). Down through the years, we have seen some Covenant Theologians accept the premillennial position, but most Reformers continued to be Postmillennialists or Amillennialists. This was due to the fact they continued to hold to an allegorical interpretation of prophecy and the supposition/imposition that God had *cast away* the nation of Israel and replaced national Israel with the state church and the priesthood of Israel with *clergymen*. Therefore, their heretical Ecclesiology determined and influenced their Eschatology. Reformed Theology continued to be primarily

Roman Catholic (Augustinian) in their Eschatology (primarily Preterism).

The Reformation's Soteriological reforms were not greatly different than Augustine's. There were some new developments by Ulrich Zwingli, Menno Simmons, Jacob Arminius, and a few others, but the central position was that God has *chosen* certain people to be saved while the rest of humanity was relegated to reprobation. This position has been divided into as many different streams as there are different people holding it the position.

When questions arise concerning these variations, Reformed Theologians always return to Augustine or Calvin as their standards of orthodoxy. They interpret Scripture from the statements of these men and their interpretation of what those statements mean (i.e., *this is what they really meant*), not necessarily merely upon what the Scriptures say apart from Augustine's or Calvin's comments. Then, if this referral to Augustine or Calvin does not provide enough weight to their theological arguments, they will quote other noted *Reformed scholars* who give another variation of explanation from a *Reformed perspective*. Answering the many objections to their positions is done by merely quoting a *proof text* upon which their presupposition has been imposed demanding submission to their presupposition.

My purpose in authoring this book is not to merely refute the presuppositions of Calvinism, Arminianism, and Covenant Theology, but to question the very methodology that results in these *systemic theologies*. The *systemic theologies* known as Calvinism, Arminianism, and Covenant Theology are all *logical systems* of theology (*Theo-logical* conclusive statements). As *logical systems* of theology, they are built upon the foundation of logical presuppositions and *proof-texts*. **In other words, these *logical systems* of theology are**

primarily based upon *eisegesis* (*reading an idea into Scripture*), not Biblical *exegesis* (*coming out of Scripture*). *Logical* and usually *philosophical presuppositions* are imposed upon the interpretation of various Bible texts resulting in distorting pure Biblical *exegesis*. These nuances are what differentiates between *systematic theologies* and mere *systemic theologies*.

The central presupposition imposed upon the Scriptures is that God has *chosen* or *elected* certain individuals to salvation and all others to eternal condemnation (*Predestination also called Sovereign Grace*). Although there are considerable variations in the presuppositions between Calvinism and Arminianism (and many more variations between those holding to these two positions), the purpose here is to seek to show that these presuppositions (TULIP) are NO WHERE to be found in the Scriptures. God has not *elected* anyone to be saved (to salvation) or anyone to be eternally condemned. *Election* has little, or nothing, to do with either salvation or condemnation.

The Poisoned TULIP

Chapter One
The Corporate/Vocational View of Election
Election as Defined by the Hermeneutic Principle of First Mention

The Apostle Paul pens the words of II Timothy 2:14-18 to his "son in the faith" Timothy. These few verses are incredibly important and certainly define the main responsibility of the faithful pastor/teacher. **One cannot teach correct doctrine if one does not know correct doctrine.** Paul had been a *master* of Judaism's false teachings of the Mosaic Covenant. Paul's beliefs regarding the doctrine of salvation and the doctrine of grace were certainly completely wrong. He knew the Old Testament Scriptures in detail. However, like most of the *master teachers* of Israel – Nicodemus and the Sanhedrin. Yet, Paul had it all wrong. When Paul pens the words of II Timothy 2:14-18, he writes them with the shame of his past ignorance burning in his heart.

How many had Paul deceived in the past with his false teachings of Judaism? The weight of having taught some false doctrine(s) burdened the heart of the man of God after learning right doctrine. Surely this must have been a great torture to Paul's heart. Surely Paul would want to caution the preachers that would follow him in the generations of the future about "rightly dividing the Word of truth." This is a great burden on those with a heart for God. **Laboring "in the Word and doctrine" (I Timothy 5:17) is essential because we reproduce what we believe in those we teach.** God's instructive and cautionary words of II Timothy 2:15 from God through Paul to Timothy and thereby to us down through the centuries are incredibly and critically important words.

"¹⁴ Of these things put *them* in remembrance, charging *them* before the Lord that they strive not about words to no profit, *but* to the subverting of the hearers. ¹⁵ **Study**

to shew thyself approved unto God, a workman that needeth not to be ashamed, rightly dividing the word of truth. [16] But shun profane *and* vain babblings: for they will increase unto more ungodliness. [17] And their word will eat as doth a canker: of whom is Hymenaeus and Philetus; [18] Who concerning the truth have erred, saying that the resurrection is past already; and overthrow the faith of some" (II Timothy 2:14-18).

There is no place for those in the ministry who are lazy students of God's Word. There is no place for those in the ministry who do not know how to gather the exact meaning of what God has said and explain that meaning through preaching/teaching. One of the qualifications of a pastor as detailed in II Timothy 2:24 is he must be "apt to teach."

"[24] And the servant of the Lord must not strive; but be gentle unto all *men*, **apt to teach, patient,** [25] In meekness instructing those that oppose themselves; if God peradventure will give them repentance to the acknowledging of the truth; [26] And *that* they may recover themselves out of the snare of the devil, who are taken captive by him at his will" (II Timothy 2:24-26).

The words "apt to teach" are translated from the Greek word *didaktikós* (did-ak-tik-os'). It is the word from which we get our English word *didactic*. The focus of didactic teaching is to slowly and meticulously ensure that the student is grasping what is being taught. The intent of didactic teaching is substantive truth that can then be reproduced through the student as he is commanded to "commit thou to faithful men, who shall be able to teach others also" (II Timothy 2:2).

Therefore, the word "patient" is added to the qualifications. Before any pastor can be "apt to teach," he

MUST BE skilled and ready to teach by careful and meticulous labor in "rightly dividing the word of truth." Therefore, the "elders {*pastors*} that rule well be counted worthy of double honour {*money paid*}, **especially they who labour in the word and doctrine**" (I Timothy 5:17). Lazy Bible students will be worthless Bible teachers and should never be allowed behind a pulpit to preach/teach.

Learning the governing principles of Biblical hermeneutics should be one of the highest priorities for any man desiring the office of a bishop. A foundational rule of Biblical interpretation is known as the *Law of First Mention*. The **1917 Edition of the Scofield Reference Bible's** introduction to the book of Genesis gives us some great insight into God's introduction to the whole of His Scriptural revelation and the purpose of that inspired revelation.

"**GENESIS** is the book of **beginnings**. It records not only the beginning of the heavens and the earth, and of plant, animal, and human life, but also of all human institutions and relationships. Typically, it speaks of the new birth, the new creation, where all was chaos and ruin. With Genesis begins also that progressive self-revelation of God which culminates in Christ. The three primary names of Deity, Elohim, Jehovah, and Adonai, and the five most important of the compound names, occur in Genesis; and that in an ordered progression which could not be changed without confusion. The problem of **sin** as affecting man's condition in the earth and his relation to God, and the divine solution of that problem are here in essence. Of the eight **great covenants** which condition human life and the divine redemption, four, the **Edenic, Adamic, Noahic, and Abrahamic Covenants** are in this book; and these are the fundamental covenants to which the other four, the **Mosaic, Palestinian, Davidic, and New Covenants**, are related chiefly as adding detail or development. Genesis enters into the very structure of the New Testament, in which it is quoted above sixty times in seventeen books. In a profound sense, therefore, **the roots of all subsequent revelation are planted deep in Genesis, and whoever would truly comprehend that revelation must begin here**. The inspiration of Genesis and its character as a divine revelation are authenticated by the testimony of Christ **Mt** 19:4-6; 24:37-39; **Mr** 10:4-9; **Lu** 11:49-51; 17:26-29,32. Genesis is in five chief divisions:

I. Creation (1. 1-2.25)
II. The fall and redemption (3. 1-4, 7).
III. The Diverse Seeds, Cain and Seth, to the Flood (4.8-7.24).
IV. The Flood to Babel (8.1-11.9).
V. From the call of Abram to the death of Joseph (11:10-50:26).

The events recorded in Genesis cover a period of 2,315 years (Ussher)."[3] (Underlining added)

Although Scofield lays the foundations for his erroneous *Gap Theory* in this statement, he is accurately establishing a critical truth to Biblical hermeneutics in this introduction to the book of Genesis in the statement: **"In a profound sense, therefore, the roots of all subsequent revelation are planted deep in Genesis, and whoever would truly comprehend that revelation must begin here."**

---

[3] SCOFIELD REFERENCE NOTES (Old Scofield 1917 Edition), SwordSearcher 4.8 software

The Hermeneutical Law of First Mention

Often people give meaning to words that are not consistent with God's original and contextual use (especially readers that begin reading the Bible without Old Testament foundations of understanding). **The *Law of First Mention* understands that every *doctrine* of Scripture in its simplest form finds its origin in the book of Genesis.** The *Law of First Mention* requires the person seeking to "rightly divide the word of truth" begin with the first mention of any doctrine in the Bible to discover the fundamental meaning inherent in that first occurrence. **Although later occurrences may add clarity, meaning, definition or extension, the later occurrences will never change the original meaning to be different from the original intent.** The original meaning is always present within the later occurrence. The fundamental truth of the *original occurrence* will always be the dominant meaning. The doctrine may expand in clarity and definition, but it will never change in that God's does not change. This will be especially important as we look at God's *choosing/election* in the Old Testament books.

We must caution here against *monothetic definitions* of words. Although there are certain things innate to a word in the definition of that word, there are also variations to that definition in varying contexts. Context can paint different word pictures. For instance, the phrase, *see the boy running* paints a different picture than the phrase, *my egg is runny.* Both are derivatives of the same word *run,* but the use in different contexts radically change the word portrait before us.

A second caution is against the tendency to begin our understanding of Old Testament books from the context of our understanding the New Testament writings. There is a tendency to interpret the Old Testament from the New Testament rather than interpreting the New Testament from the already established truths of the Old Testament. There may be *mysteries* that are obscure in the Old Testament books that are revealed in the New Testament books, but generally we interpret the New Testament books from the Old Testament. Although the New Testament may *clarify* what the Old Testament teaches, it never contradicts what the Old Testament teaches.

The etymological definition of a word can only truly be determined by "discovering the meaning of the word inductively."[4] Why is this true? Because God has said, "For I am the LORD, **I change not . . .**" (Malachi 3:6).

"Every good gift and every perfect gift is from above, and cometh down from the Father of lights, **with whom is no variableness, neither shadow of turning**" (James 1:17).

The Hermeneutical Law of Recurrence

The hermeneutical *Law of Recurrence* is an inseparable partner to the *Law of First Mention.* Often in the Bible, we find a new historical account of something previously revealed in Scripture. The repetition of such an account may give added details that the previous account did not provide. Each mention of such historical events, doctrines, or word use must be carefully researched to discover the context and if added details are provided. This is also known as an *inductive methodology* (not to be confused with *deductive/inductive logic*). An accurate understanding will come when we gather all the Scriptural evidence to a particular subject or doctrine. This *process* is

---

[4] Exegetical Fallacies; D.A. Carson, Baker Bookhouse

what defines a doctrine and what allows the exegete to become dogmatic about any given subject or doctrine.

An *inductive methodology* reasons from parts to the whole, from particulars to the general; a conclusion is drawn from the weight of *all* the evidence. An *inductive methodology* is primary to avoiding *eisegesis* (reading a presupposition *into* what the Bible is saying). Systematic theologies are conclusive and dogmatic statements based upon the weight of Scriptural evidence concluded through the inductive *exegesis* (extracting what God is saying *out of* what the Bible says) of *every* Bible text relating to that theological statement. This is categorically different than *Proof Texting* or a *deductive methodology*.

When all these *checks and balances* are carefully applied to every text and our *correct* understanding of various texts are added together, we can be confident we have determined what God wants us to know. In other words, it can be said that the Word of God has been "rightly divided." If we have contradictions between texts, we have an error in our *exegesis* somewhere. *Harmony of truth* must exist before we can claim to have a true systematic theology because God is not the author of confusion.

Applying the Laws of First Mention and Recurrence to the Doctrine of Election

If we want to understand God's choosing or electing according to His sovereign purpose, we must begin with the *first occurrence* in its use in Scripture (the *Law of First Mention*) and build inductively from that point forward. In this inductive approach, we should be able to discover a common meaning if a common meaning occurs consistently in the Scriptures (the *Law of Recurrence*).

Exegesis is interpreting, understanding, and exacting the meaning of what God has said in the inspired Words of Scripture from the grammar/syntax of Scripture applying the rules of Biblical interpretation (hermeneutics) to the text. Finding the beginning teaching of a word's use in Scripture to discover the beginning teaching on any doctrine from that word's use and the meaning of that word's use is applying the Law of First Mention. Then, finding later uses of that same word, or derivatives of that word, in historical context is applying the Law of Recurrence.

The most common word translated "chosen" in the Old Testament books is the Hebrew word *bachar* (baw-khar'). There appears to be two parallel ideas communicated using this word: *to choose* and *to test*. The key word in the criterion of God's *choice* is that God's calling/election is "according to *His* purpose" (Romans 8:28). *The Theological Workbook of the Old Testament* makes the following comment on the meaning of the word *bachar* (baw-khar').

". . . [T]he word is used to express that choosing which has ultimate and eternal significance. On the one hand God chooses a people (Ps 135:4), certain tribes (Ps 78:68), specific individuals (I Kings 8:16; I Chr 28:5; I Sam 10:24; II Sam 6:21), and a place for his name (Deut 12:25; etc.). **In all these cases serviceability rather than simple arbitrariness is at the heart of choosing.** Thus, Yahweh chose Israel to be holy and thereby to serve as his witnesses among the nations (Duet 14:6)."[5] (Bolding added)

---

[5] R. Laird Harris, Gleason L. Archer, Jr., and Bruce K. Waltke, The Theological Workbook of the Old Testament, Vol. I, Moody Bible Institute of Chicago, page 100.

In an inductive evaluation of the use of the Hebrew word *bachar* (baw-khar'), it is apparent that the purpose of God's choosing is *vocational service, ministry, or a specific task.* The word always carries with it *vocational connotations* (not salvational; Ephesians 4:1). This is the common usage regarding God's *electing* throughout Scripture.

Innumerable Scriptural examples in *recurring* usage bear testimony to this common meaning. Since this election is vocational, "called according to *his* purpose" (Romans 8:28), and not salvational, and since God selects certain groups and individuals for specific tasks, He can unselect them if they fail in His covenant requirements and He can then select others, or another, to fulfill His purpose. This is what happened with the Mosaic Covenant priesthood of Israel (Malachi chapters 2 and 3; compare Romans chapter 11).

None of the covenants carry salvational connotations or conditions. All the covenants are with God's *elect.* In other words, at the beginning of each new dispensation God *elected* a remnant of people who were already believers and *then* made covenants with those He *elected.* Although some covenants are conditional for God's blessings, none of the covenants are conditional for salvation.

The first two uses of the word "chosen" in the Bible are used regarding the *vocational choice* of Aaron as High Priest (Numbers 16:4) and God's choice of the children of Israel (*corporately as a group*) to be His *chosen people* (Deuteronomy 7:1-11). **God's *purpose* for this choosing is the transference of inspired revelation and knowledge of God to maintain a continuum of a faithful remnant of believers from generation to generation.** This transference of inspired revelation and knowledge of God was to maintain a faithful remnant of believers through which Messiah would be born. The *Law of First Mention* and an inductive methodology direct us to understand that this is the way the word "chosen" (*election*) is to be understood throughout Scripture. ***If this is true*, we should be able to conclusively show that this is the common usage of the term and the common meaning through the *Law of Recurrence*.**

The question we must ask ourselves is <u>if</u>, in God's choice of the nation of Israel, the salvation of individuals is implied or presumed? This question will be answered in some detail in later chapters as we look at Romans chapters eight through eleven. **Certainly, Romans chapter nine alone shows that the salvation of individual Jews was not part of the corporate election of the nation of Israel.** We must also look at this as it unfolds in Scripture to see if salvation is implied or presumed in any recurrence (the *Law of Recurrence*).

"[6] Not as though the word of God hath taken none effect. For they *are* not all Israel, which are of Israel: [7] Neither, because they are the seed of Abraham, *are they* all children: but, In Isaac shall thy seed be called. [8] That is, They which are the children of the flesh, these *are* not the children of God: **but the children of the promise** {*faith in the promised Messiah, Galatians 3:16*} **are counted for the seed**" (Romans 9:6-8).

The use of the word "chosen" in the Old Testament books is *almost always* used to refer to the choice of groups and only occasionally to individuals. The *exceptions* would be the references that refer to Messiah, individual prophets chosen by God, individual kings chosen by God, or Mary chosen by God to be the birthmother of Jesus. The word "chosen" is also used in the

Old Testament books to refer to the city of Jerusalem or Mt. Zion (Deuteronomy 16:11). **However, there does not appear to be even one occurrence in the Old Testament books where the word "chosen" is** *ever* **used to refer to individuals elected to be** *saved.*

The word "elect" in the Old Testament Scriptures is from the Hebrew word *bachiyr* (baw-kheer'; used 13 times in the O.T.[6]). It is the noun form of *bachar* (baw-khar'; used 164 times in O.T.[7]). *Bachiyr* (baw-kheer') is used of the Messiah (Isaiah 42:1) and the nation of Israel (descendants of Jacob; Isaiah 45:4; 65:9 and 65:22). **Again, the word is never used to refer to someone chosen/elected to be** *saved.*

The following portions of Scripture are intended to be representative (not exhaustive, of the uses of the word "chosen" as translated from the Hebrew word *bachar* (baw-khar') as defined above (although an exhaustive study has been done, it will not be presented here due to space). **The following use of** *chosen* **in recurring texts inductively reveal that God's** *choosing* **is always** *vocational* **in scope and never** *salvational* **in scope.**

In these many Scriptures it becomes apparent very quickly that the word "chosen" is not used in the context of electing anyone to be saved. People and groups of people were chosen to further God's purposes. Some individuals would get saved through their decision in faith and God would impute to them His righteousness (justification), but no one was chosen to be saved. Most of the children of Israel did not get saved (Romans 9:6-8).

The Children of Israel as a Nation of People were Chosen Corporately.

---

[6] King James Version Strong's Exhaustive Concordance Links, SwordSearcher 4.8 Software.
[7] Ibid

"[1] When the LORD thy God shall bring thee into the land whither thou goest to possess it, and hath cast out many nations before thee, the Hittites, and the Girgashites, and the Amorites, and the Canaanites, and the Perizzites, and the Hivites, and the Jebusites, **seven nations greater and mightier than thou**; [2] And when the LORD thy God shall deliver them before thee; thou shalt smite them, *and* utterly destroy them; thou shalt make no covenant with them, nor shew mercy unto them: [3] Neither shalt thou make marriages with them; thy daughter thou shalt not give unto his son, nor his daughter shalt thou take unto thy son. [4] For they will turn away thy son from following me, that they may serve other gods: so will the anger of the LORD be kindled against you, and destroy thee suddenly. [5] But thus shall ye deal with them; ye shall destroy their altars, and break down their images, and cut down their groves, and burn their graven images with fire. [6] For thou *art* **an holy people** unto the LORD thy God: the **LORD thy God hath chosen thee** {*corporately*} **to be a special people unto himself**, above all people that *are* upon the face of the earth. [7] The LORD did not set his love upon you, nor choose you, because ye were more in number than any people; for ye *were* the fewest of all people: [8] But because the LORD loved you, and **because he would keep the oath which he had sworn unto your fathers**, hath the LORD brought you out with a mighty hand, and **redeemed** {*corporate redemption of the nation of Israel out of Egyptian bondage; this is not salvational*} you out of the house of bondmen, from the hand of Pharaoh king of Egypt. [9] Know therefore that the LORD thy God, he *is* God, the faithful God, which keepeth covenant and mercy with them that love him and keep his commandments to a thousand generations; [10] And repayeth them that hate him to their face, to destroy them: he will not be slack to him that hateth him, he will repay him to his face. [11] Thou shalt therefore keep the commandments, and the statutes, and the judgments, which I command thee this day, to do them" (Deuteronomy 7:1-11).

"[1] Ye *are* the children of the LORD your God: ye shall not cut yourselves, nor make any baldness between your eyes for the dead. [2] For thou *art* an holy people unto the LORD thy God, and **the LORD hath chosen thee to be a peculiar people unto himself,** above all the nations that *are* upon the earth" (Deuteronomy 14:1-2).

"[13] O ye seed of Israel his servant, ye children of Jacob, **his chosen ones.** [14] He *is* the LORD our God; his judgments *are* in all the earth" (I Chronicles 16:13-14).

"Blessed *is* **the nation** whose God *is* the LORD; *and* **the people** *whom* he hath chosen for his own inheritance" (Psalm 33:12).

The Tribe of Levi as the Old Covenant Priesthood Chosen Corporately

The second category of corporate election is God choosing the tribe of Levi to be His priests. Again, salvation is neither implied nor presumed in choosing the men of the tribe of Levi to be God's priests. This category is especially important to understand corporate and vocational election in the New Covenant Church and the Melchizedekian priesthood of all Church Age believers. The corporate and vocational election in the New Covenant Church and the Melchizedekian priesthood of all Church Age believers is the substance of the Epistle to the Ephesians. Calvinism has completely warped the understanding of the epistle to the Ephesians into individual election to salvation. This is false and completely distorts the teaching of this epistle (Ephesians 4:1). This is the primary way election is used throughout the New Testament.

"¹ The **priests the Levites, *and* all the tribe of Levi, shall have no part nor inheritance with Israel: they shall eat the offerings** of the LORD made by fire, and his inheritance *{as their portion for their physical sustenance}*. ² Therefore shall they have no inheritance among their brethren: the LORD *is* their inheritance, as he hath said unto them. ³ And **this shall be the priest's due from the people**, from them that offer a sacrifice, whether *it be* ox or sheep; and **they shall give unto the priest the shoulder, and the two cheeks, and the maw.** ⁴ The firstfruit *also* of thy corn, of thy wine, and of thine oil, and the first of the fleece of thy sheep, shalt thou give him. ⁵ **For the LORD thy God hath chosen him** *{the priest}* **out of all thy tribes**, to stand to minister in the name of the LORD, **him and his sons** for ever" (Deuteronomy 18:1-5).

"And the priests the sons of Levi shall come near; **for them the LORD thy God hath chosen to minister unto him**, and to bless in the name of the LORD; and **by their word shall every controversy and every stroke be *tried*:**" (Deuteronomy 21:5).

God Chose the Kings and Prophets for His Vocational Purposes

Sometimes God chose and gave the children of Israel the kind of king they wanted. Saul was such a choice for Israel. Saul's salvation is certainly questionable even though it is said that "God gave him another heart" (I Samuel 10:9). For the Calvinist, this verse of Scripture is said to mean Saul was regenerated and saved without any act of faith upon his part. This is a highly questionable interpretation of these few words. This does not mean Saul was not a saved man, justified by grace through faith. The point is that the statement "thou shalt be turned into another man" in I Samuel 10:6 simply means Saul was turned from being a husbandman to being a prophet and a king. He had no heart for being a prophet and king, so God gave him "another heart" (I Samuel 10:9) for these two new vocational callings in his life.

Context would give us another meaning vastly different than Saul being regenerated. The context is to show Saul that God had chosen him (I Samuel 10:1) as he was anointed by the prophet Samuel to be king. Saul was not yet convinced. Saul was a husbandman and certainly had no qualifications to lead a nation. The inclination of Saul's heart was towards agriculture and husbandry. Saul had no inclinations to be either a king or a prophet. It would be presuppositional to read any more into this text than this understanding from the context. There is no implication in God choosing a man to be king that the person is saved. Just as Abraham was chosen by God to be the father of national Israel before Abraham was justified by grace through faith, lost kings may have been chosen (elected) by God to be kings before they get saved. Some individuals chosen to be kings may never have gotten saved. Being saved was not a requirement of God's choosing (Romans 13:1).

"And **Samuel said** to all the people, **See ye him whom the LORD hath chosen**, that *there is* none like him {*Saul*} among all the people? And all the people shouted, and said, God save the king" (I Samuel 10:24).

"[10] Again, Jesse made seven of his sons to pass before Samuel. And Samuel said unto Jesse, **The LORD hath not chosen these.** [11] And Samuel said unto Jesse, Are here all *thy* children? And he said, There remaineth yet the youngest {*David*}, and, behold, he keepeth the sheep. And Samuel said unto Jesse, Send and fetch him: for we will not sit down till he come hither. ¹² And he sent, and brought him in. Now he *was* ruddy, *and* withal of a beautiful countenance, and goodly to look to. And the LORD said, **Arise, anoint him: for this *is* he**. ¹³ Then Samuel took the horn of oil, and anointed him in the midst of his brethren: and the Spirit of the LORD came upon David from that day forward. So Samuel rose up, and went to Ramah" (I Samuel 16:10-13).

I Kings 8:22-53 records Solomon's prayer of dedication for the temple he had built for the Lord. From the words of this prayer, it would certainly appear that Solomon was a saved man. However, this would be an assumption. **Solomon might have been a saved man who leaped into carnality later, and then late in his life repented and began living for the Lord. We are not told that Solomon was justified by faith at this time of his life. He may have been, but we are not told he was.** There are many deeply religious and articulate men who are lost. Nicodemus of John chapter three would be such an example. Solomon may have been a saved man, but the testimony of most of his life was that he was more of a pagan than a believer. This is his own testimony about himself and his life in the book God used him to pen called Ecclesiastes. It does appear that Solomon became a believer, but the practical testimony of most of his life is that of an unbeliever.

"⁷ And now, O LORD my God, **thou hast made thy servant king** {*Solomon*} instead of David my father: and I *am but* a little child: I know not *how* to go out or come in. ⁸ And thy servant *is* **in the midst of thy people which thou hast chosen**, a great people, that cannot be numbered nor counted for multitude. ⁹ **Give therefore thy servant an understanding heart** to judge thy people, that I may discern between good and bad: for who is able to judge this thy so great a people‖ (I Kings 3:7-9)?

The City of Jerusalem as God's Chosen Place on Planet Earth

"‖⁴⁴ If thy people go out to battle against their enemy, whithersoever thou shalt send them, and shall pray unto the LORD **toward the city which thou hast chosen**, and *toward* the house that I have built for thy name: ⁴⁵ Then hear thou in heaven their prayer and their supplication, and maintain their cause" (I Kings 8:44-45; see also verse 48; 11:13, 32 and, 36).

The Tribe of Judah Chosen as the Tribe of Messiah and His Eternal Reign

"‖² Then David the king stood up upon his feet, and said, Hear me, my brethren, and my people: *As for me*, I *had* in mine heart to build an house of rest for the ark of the covenant of the LORD, and for the footstool of our God, and had made ready for the building: ³ But God said unto me, Thou shalt not build an house for my name, because thou *hast been* a man of war, and hast shed blood. ⁴ Howbeit the LORD God of Israel chose me before all the house of my father to be king over Israel for ever: **for he hath chosen Judah *to be* the ruler**; and of the house of Judah, the house of my father; and among the sons of my father he liked me to make *me* king over all Israel: ⁵ And of all my sons, (for the LORD hath given me many sons,) **he hath chosen Solomon my son to sit upon the throne of the kingdom of the**

LORD over Israel. [6] And he said unto me, **Solomon thy son, he shall build my house and my courts: for I have chosen him** *to be* **my son, and I will be his father.** [7] Moreover I will establish his kingdom for ever, if he be constant to do my commandments and my judgments, as at this day" (I Chronicles 28:2-7).

"[3] I have **made a covenant with my chosen**, I have sworn unto **David my servant**, [4] Thy seed will I establish for ever, and build up thy throne to all generations. Selah" (Psalm 89:3-4).

There is conclusive and dogmatic evidence from the Old Testament Scriptures that God's choosing (election) is always used to refer to God's *vocational* **choices to fulfill His purposes.** God's choosing is never used in the sense that God chose someone to be saved from condemnation. It can readily be shown that this meaning is consistent with God's use of these terms in the New Testaments books as well.

Corporate and Vocational Election in the New Testament Books

The primary word translated "chose," "chosen," and "choice" in the New Testament books is the Greek word *eklegomai* (ek-leg'-om-ahee). The word "elect" is translated from the Greek word *eklektos* (ek-lek-tos'), of which *eklegomai* is a derivative. The *Law of First Mention* should result in the same categories of use in the New Testament books as those we find in the Old Testament books. We cannot read election to salvation into any New Testament Scripture.

The Children of Israel
Elect as a Nation of People (not as saved people)

"[14] But when ye shall see the abomination of desolation, spoken of by Daniel the prophet, standing where it ought not, (let him that readeth understand,) then let them that be in Judaea flee to the mountains: [15] And let him that is on the housetop not go down into the house, neither enter *therein*, to take any thing out of his house: [16] And let him that is in the field not turn back again for to take up his garment. [17] But woe to them that are with child, and to them that give suck in those days! [18] And pray ye that your flight be not in the winter. [19] For *in* those days shall be affliction, such as was not from the beginning of the creation which God created unto this time, neither shall be. [20] And except that the Lord had shortened those days, no flesh should be saved: **but for the elect's sake** {*Israel during the seven-year Tribulation prior to the second coming*}, **whom he hath chosen, he hath shortened the days.** [21] And then if any man shall say to you, Lo, here *is* Christ; or, lo, *he is* there; believe *him* not: [22] For false Christs and false prophets shall rise, and shall shew signs and wonders, to seduce, if *it were* possible, even the elect" (Mark 13:14-22).

The Church Age believers vocationally Elect
as the Future New Covenant Priesthood
of Israel during the Millennial Kingdom

"[15] Henceforth I call you not servants; for the servant knoweth not what his lord doeth: but I have called you friends; for all things that I have heard of my Father I have made known unto you. [16] **Ye have not chosen me, but I have chosen you**, and ordained you, that ye should go and bring forth fruit, and *that* your fruit should remain: that whatsoever ye shall ask of the Father in my name, he may give it you. [17] These things I command you, that ye love one another" (John 15:15-17; *although these words are spoken to the apostles, their application is for all believers*).

"[26] For ye see your calling, brethren, how that not many wise men after the flesh, not many mighty, not many noble, *are called*: [27] But **God hath chosen the foolish things of the world to confound the wise; and God hath chosen the weak things of the world to confound the things which are mighty; [28] And base things of the world, and things which are despised, hath God chosen, *yea*, and things which are not, to bring to nought things that are**: [29] That no flesh should glory in his presence. [30] **But of him are ye in Christ Jesus**, who of God is made unto us wisdom, and righteousness, and sanctification, and redemption: [31] That, according as it is written, He that glorieth, let him glory in the Lord" (I Corinthians 1:26-31).

The epistle to the Ephesians, especially its first chapter, is a favorite proof text for the Calvinist to show individual election to salvation. However, to reach that conclusion the Calvinist must read the presupposition that election is to salvation into the text. The context of the epistle is the vocational election of all Church Age believers corporately as the new priesthood after the order of Melchisedec with Christ as the "head" or High Priest.

Ephesians Chapter One Outline

Notice that every pronoun in Ephesians chapter one referring to believers is plural. This is evident in the KJV, but not all other English translations. This is important in that the *election* ("chosen," Ephesians 1: 4) of Ephesians chapter one is the *election* of the Church corporately to be a new priesthood. It is not the *election* of individuals to be saved. Election is *vocational*, not *salvational*.

1. The Church is a corporation of "saints" (sanctified priests) as "born again" believers faithful to the commands of Jesus Christ (Ephesians 1:1).

2. The Church is distinct from the nation of Israel and her blessings are eternal and spiritual rather than temporal and earthly (Ephesians 1:3).

3. The Church is chosen corporately "in Christ," her High Priest, as a new, spiritual Priesthood before "the foundation of the world" (i.e., not an afterthought, but a *before creation thought*, Ephesians 1:4).

4. This whole new priesthood, which is "saved by grace through faith," is predestined to glorification (Ephesians 1:5).   This is the meaning of the word "adoption" – translated from the Greek *huiothesia* (hwee-oth-es-ee'-ah). The word means the placement or position of the sons of God. This cannot be understood apart from the placement of the "firstborn" as the typical priesthood now fulfilled in the Church as the priesthood of all believers in the "church of the firstborn" (Hebrews 12:23).

5. This new priesthood is "accepted" (positionally sanctified and consecrated) in Christ, "the beloved" (Ephesians 1:6-9).

6. The Church is embryonically what all believers of all Ages will be in "the regeneration" in the new Heaven/Earth – a kingdom of glorified priests (Ephesians 1:10-14).

7. Paul's prayer for the *enabling power* of the indwelling *Christ-life* of the believer's High Priest is to be realized, actuated, and released in and through the local church as the "body" of Christ (Ephesians 1:15-23).

As the first chapter of Ephesians is read, carefully note the plural pronouns. Then bring to the chapter the inductive understanding of the word "chosen" already established from the laws of *First Mention* and *Recurrence* from the Old Testament. Cleary from the Old Testament, God never elected anyone to be saved. God chose Abraham to be the father the nation of Israel. God chose Moses to lead them out of Egyptian bondage and to establish them under the Mosaic Covenant. God chose the tribe of Levi to be His priests. God chose Joshua to lead the children of Israel into the promised land. God chose Saul, David, and Solomon to be the first kings of Israel. God also chose prophets. **Salvation is never implied in the choosing of anyone!**

All Church Age saints are "called" to serve as a holy priesthood before God with Jesus as our heavenly High Priest. This is Melchizedekian "order," not the Levitical order (Hebrews 5:6, 10, 6:20, 7:11, 15, 17, and 21). **New Testament election is all Church Age believers (the *Church*) chosen to be priests.** As Paul says in II Timothy 1:9, "Who hath saved us, and **called *us* with an holy calling, not according to our works, but according to his own purpose and grace**, which was given us in Christ Jesus before the world began." Paul says the same also in Ephesians 1:11.

"[1] Paul, an apostle of Jesus Christ by the will of God, **to the saints** {*the corporate entity called the Church*} which are at Ephesus, and to the faithful in Christ Jesus: [2] Grace *be* to you, and peace, from God our Father, and *from* the Lord Jesus Christ. [3] Blessed *be* the God and Father of our Lord Jesus Christ, who hath blessed **us** {*the corporate entity called the Church*} with all spiritual blessings in heavenly *places* in Christ: [4] **According as he hath chosen us** {*the corporate entity called the Church*} **in him before the foundation of the world,** that **we** {*the corporate entity called the*

Church} should be holy and without blame before him in love: [5] Having predestinated **us** {*the corporate entity called the Church*} unto the adoption of children by Jesus Christ to himself, according to the good pleasure of his will, [6] To the praise of the glory of his grace, wherein he hath made **us** {*the corporate entity called the Church*} accepted in the beloved. [7] In whom **we** {*the corporate entity called the Church*} have redemption through his blood, the forgiveness of sins, according to the riches of his grace; [8] Wherein he hath abounded toward **us** {*the corporate entity called the Church*} in all wisdom and prudence; [9] Having made known unto **us** {*the corporate entity called the Church*} the mystery of his will, according to his good pleasure which he hath purposed in himself: [10] That in the dispensation of the fulness of times he might gather together in one all things in Christ, both which are in heaven, and which are on earth; *even* in him: [11] In whom also **we** {*the corporate entity called the Church*} have obtained an inheritance, **being predestinated according to the purpose of him who worketh all things after the counsel of his own will**: [12] That **we** {*the corporate entity called the Church*} should be to the praise of his glory, who first trusted in Christ. [13] In whom **ye** also *trusted*, after that **ye** heard the word of truth, the gospel of your salvation: in whom also after that **ye** believed, **ye** were sealed with that holy Spirit of promise, [14] Which is the earnest of **our** {*the corporate entity called the Church*} inheritance until the redemption of the purchased possession, unto the praise of his glory" (Ephesians 1:1-14; *this is addressed to the Church at Ephesus and speaks to that group collective and to the Church as all New Covenant believers*).

"[4] To whom coming, *as unto* a living stone, disallowed indeed of men, but **chosen of God**, *and* precious, [5] Ye also {*the corporate entity called the Church*}, as lively stones, are built up a spiritual house, **an holy priesthood**, to offer up spiritual sacrifices, acceptable to God by Jesus Christ. [6] Wherefore also it is contained in the scripture, Behold, I lay in Sion a chief corner stone, elect, precious: and he that believeth on him shall not be confounded. [7] Unto you therefore which believe *he is* precious: but unto them which be disobedient {*the Mosaic Covenant priesthood*}, the stone which the builders disallowed, the same is made the head of the corner, [8] And a stone of stumbling, and a rock of offence, *even to them* which stumble at the word, being disobedient: whereunto also they were appointed. [9] **But ye** {*the corporate entity called the Church*} **are a chosen generation, a royal priesthood**, an holy nation, a peculiar people; that ye should shew forth the praises of him who hath called you out of darkness into his marvellous light: [10] Which in time past *were* not a people, but *are* now the people of God: which had not obtained mercy, but now have obtained mercy"(I Peter 2:4-10).

"These shall make war with the Lamb, and the Lamb shall overcome them: for he is Lord of lords, and King of kings: and **they** {*the corporate entity called the Church*} **that are with him** *are* **called, and chosen, and faithful**" (Revelation 17:14).

God's Individual Vocational Choice/Calling of Prophets, Evangelists, and Pastors

"[13] And when it was day, he called *unto him* his disciples: and of them **he chose twelve**, whom also he named apostles; ¹⁴ Simon, (whom he also named Peter,) and Andrew his brother, James and John, Philip and Bartholomew, ¹⁵ Matthew and Thomas, James the *son* of Alphaeus, and Simon called Zelotes, ¹⁶ And Judas *the brother* of James, and Judas Iscariot, which also was the traitor" (Luke 6:13-16; *notice Judas Iscariot was one of the chosen, but was not saved*).

"⁶⁷ Then said Jesus unto the twelve, Will ye also go away? ⁶⁸ Then Simon Peter answered him, Lord, to whom shall we go? thou hast the words of eternal life. ⁶⁹ And we believe and are sure that thou art that Christ, the Son of the living God. ⁷⁰ Jesus answered them, **Have not I chosen you twelve**, and one of you is a devil? ⁷¹ He spake of Judas Iscariot *the son* of Simon: for he it was that should betray him, being one of the twelve" (John 6:67-71).

"¹⁸ I speak not of you all: **I know whom I have chosen**: but that the scripture may be fulfilled, He that eateth bread with me hath lifted up his heel against me. ¹⁹ Now I tell you before it come, that, when it is come to pass, ye may believe that I am *he*" (John 13:18-19; *notice Jesus had a purpose in choosing Judas Iscariot and that, although Judas was chosen, he was not saved*).

"¹ The former treatise have I made, O Theophilus, of all that Jesus began both to do and teach, ² Until the day in which he was taken up, after that he through the Holy Ghost had given commandments unto **the apostles whom he had chosen**:" (Acts 1:1-2).

"²³ And they appointed two, Joseph called Barsabas, who was surnamed Justus, and Matthias. ²⁴ And they prayed, and said, Thou, Lord, which knowest the hearts of all *men*, **shew whether of these two thou hast chosen**, [25] That he may **take part of this ministry and apostleship**, from which Judas by transgression fell, that he might go to his own place. [26] And they gave forth their lots; and the lot fell upon Matthias; and he was numbered with the eleven apostles" (Acts 1:23-26; *note: this was not God's choosing*).

The City of Jerusalem as God's Chosen Place on Planet Earth

"And I looked, and, lo, a Lamb **stood on the mount Sion** {*Jerusalem*}, and with him an hundred forty *and* four thousand {*God's sealed evangelist to preach salvation by grace through faith in Jesus to the Jews during the Tribulation*}, having his Father's name written in their foreheads" (Revelation 14:1).

The New Testament Confirms what the Old Testament Affirms; the New Testament Confirms Judah as the Elect Tribe of the Messiah

The New Testament books confirm what the Old Testament books teach. This is usually just recurrence of what has been taught aforehand. Sometimes new information is added in recurrence texts. Acts 13:16-23 is a recurrence text in the New Testament confirming what was taught in the Old Testament.

"[16] Then Paul stood up, and beckoning with *his* hand said, Men of Israel, and ye that fear God, give audience. [17] **The God of this people of Israel chose our fathers**, and exalted the people when they dwelt as strangers in the land of Egypt, and with an high arm brought he them out of it. [18] And about the time of forty years suffered he their manners in the wilderness. [19] And when he had destroyed seven nations in the land of Chanaan {*early name for Palestine*}, he divided their land to them by lot. [20] And after that he gave *unto them* judges about the space of four hundred and fifty years, until Samuel the prophet. [21] And afterward they desired a king: and God gave unto them Saul the son of Cis, a man of the tribe of Benjamin, by the space of forty years. [22] And when he had removed him, he raised up unto them David to be their king; to whom also he gave testimony, and said, I have found David the *son* of Jesse, a man after mine own heart, which shall fulfil all my will. [23] **Of this man's seed hath God according to *his* promise raised unto Israel a Saviour, Jesus**" (Acts 13:16-23).

"[5] And one of the elders saith unto me, Weep not: behold, **the Lion of the tribe of Juda, the Root of David,** hath prevailed to open the book, and to loose the seven seals thereof. [6] And I beheld, and, lo, in the midst of the throne and of the four beasts, and in the midst of the elders, stood a Lamb as it had been slain, having seven horns and seven eyes, which are the seven Spirits of God sent forth into all the earth. [7] And he came and took the book out of the right hand of him that sat upon the throne" (Revelation 5:5-7).

God *vocationally choosing* groups or individuals for His sovereign purposes is contradistinctive to election being to salvation. We can clearly see from Scriptural evidence that salvation is NOT part of election. Those chosen may or may not have been saved at the time of their election or may or may not get saved after their election. This is evident by Paul's statement in Romans chapter nine.

"[1] I say the truth in Christ, I lie not, my conscience also bearing me witness in the Holy Ghost, [2] That I have great heaviness and continual sorrow in my heart. [3] For I could wish that myself were accursed from Christ for my brethren, my kinsmen according to the flesh: [4] **Who are Israelites**; to whom *pertaineth* the adoption, and the glory, and the covenants, and the giving of the law, and the service *of God*, and the promises; [5] Whose *are* the fathers, and of whom as concerning the flesh Christ *came*, who is over all, God blessed for ever. Amen. [6] Not as though the word of God hath taken none effect. **For they *are* not all Israel, which are of Israel: [7] Neither, because they are the seed of Abraham, *are they* all children: but, In Isaac shall thy seed be called. [8] That is, They which are the children of the flesh, these *are* not the children of God: but the children of the promise are counted for the seed**" (Romans 9:6-8).

Paul more thoroughly explains what he is saying about being "counted for the seed" in Galatians chapter three. Galatians 3:6-16 is defining the substance of the *faith seed* of Abraham. Faith is a choice to believe in "the Seed, which is Christ" (Galatians 3:16) to receive the gift of *God-kind righteousness* (justification).

"[6] **Even as** Abraham believed God, and it was accounted to him for righteousness. [7] **Know ye therefore that they which are of faith, the same are the children of Abraham.** [8] And the scripture, foreseeing that God would justify the heathen through faith, preached before the gospel unto Abraham, *saying*, In thee shall all nations be blessed. [9] So then they which be of faith are blessed with faithful Abraham. [10] For as many as are of the works of the law are under the curse: for it is written, Cursed *is* every one that continueth not in all things which are written in the book of the law to do them. [11] But that no man is justified by the law in the sight of God, *it is* evident: for, The just shall live by faith. [12] And the law is not of faith: but, The man that doeth them shall live in them. [13] Christ hath redeemed us from the curse of the law, being made a curse for us: for it is written, Cursed *is* every one that hangeth on a tree: [14] **That the blessing of Abraham might come on the Gentiles through Jesus Christ; that we might receive the promise of the Spirit through faith.** [15] Brethren, I speak after the manner of men; Though *it be* but a man's covenant, yet *if it be* confirmed, no man disannulleth, or addeth thereto. [16] **Now to Abraham and his seed were the promises made. He saith not, And to seeds, as of many; but as of one, And to thy seed, which is Christ**" (Galatians 3:6-16).

Was every descendent of Abraham *through the line of Jacob* **(which** *excludes Ishmael and his descendants***) one of God's elect nation (***Israel***)?** We can unequivocally say yes, without a doubt. **Was every seminal descendent of Abraham one of God's elect nation (***Israel***) saved?** We can equally and unequivocally say no, without a doubt. This is in fact the subject matter of Romans chapters nine and ten, i.e., what the seminal descendants of Abraham of the elect nation of Israel needed to do to be saved.

"[1] Brethren, my heart's desire and prayer to God for Israel is, **that they might be saved.** [2] For I bear them record that they have a zeal of God, but not according to knowledge. [3] For they **being ignorant of God's righteousness, and going about to establish their own righteousness, <u>have not submitted themselves</u> unto** the righteousness of God. [4] For Christ *is* the end of the law for righteousness **to every one that believeth**. [5] For Moses describeth the righteousness which is of the law, That the man which doeth those things shall live by them. [6] **But the righteousness which is of faith** {*justification*} **speaketh on this wise**, Say not in thine heart, Who shall ascend into heaven? (that is, to bring Christ down *from above*:) [7] Or, Who shall descend into the deep? (that is, to bring up Christ again from the dead.) [8] But what saith it {*Deuteronomy 30:14*}? The word is nigh thee, *even* in thy mouth, and in thy heart: that is, **the word of faith**, which we preach; [9] That if thou shalt confess with thy mouth the Lord Jesus, and shalt believe in thine heart that God hath raised him from the dead, thou shalt be saved. [10] For with the heart man believeth unto righteousness; and with the mouth confession is made unto salvation. [11] For the scripture saith, Whosoever believeth on him shall not be ashamed" (Romans 10:1-11).

We can see inductively from these Scriptures that the development of the doctrine of *election* in the Word of God is established by using a Scriptural overview of both the Old Testament and then recurrence in the New Testament books. This overview will be expanded upon in considerable detail later in these studies. However, **we will see that the following paragraphs summarize the doctrine of *election* in a proverbial *nutshell*.** Although this summation may appear to be complicated, it is quite simple.

The *Promised One* of Genesis 3:15 is God's Son that we know as Jesus. Jesus was chosen (*elected*) from the "foundation of the world" (Revelation 13:8) to be both the Redeemer of the lost and a new and "last Adam" (actually both the "first and the last" in that He was part of God's *Plan* before the creation of Adam, Revelation 1:17-18; I

Corinthians 15:45-50) to restore the dominion relinquished to Satan by Adam's sinful choice. The *Promised One* (the "last Adam") would be successful where the first Adam failed.

The *Promised One* would be the "firstborn" (Romans 8:29; Colossians 1:15-18) of a *New Genesis* (Matthew 19:28) and would become the "door" (John 10:1-9) into this *New Genesis* to "whosoever" of fallen humanity that are willing to believe in His death, burial, and resurrection, repent of sin, confess Him as LORD, call on Him to save them, and be supernaturally "born again" (John 3:3-7, I Peter 1:23) "by grace through faith" (Ephesians 2:8-9) into the *New Genesis* "in Christ" (I Corinthians 12:12-13; Christ now having *primogeniture* that provides inheritance of glorification into the *New Genesis;* Acts 26:18, Ephesians 1:11-18, Colossians 1:12, 3:24 and, I Peter 1:2-5).

Therefore, this whole group that would become the descendants of the *Seed* of the Promised One "through faith" (Ephesians 2:8-9) and being "born again" into "the regeneration" would become the *elect* "in Christ" (Ephesians 1:3-4, II Timothy 1:9). Although *election* does not always translate into the salvation of the individual or group *elected*, the primary and "eternal purpose" of God in *election* is a continuing and ongoing faithful remnant for the stewardship and preservation of truth to His glory to the end of time.

As we look at the *Protevangelium* of Genesis 3:15, it is important to see that the primary focus of this *first mention* of the Gospel has more to do with the restoration of dominion to mankind through the birth of the Promised One (Revelation 4:9-5:7) than it has to do with the salvation of lost souls. The salvation of lost souls is a secondary issue that is the outcome of the *crushing* of Satan's "head" (the dominion of death with which he imprisons mankind; I Corinthians 15:54-55; Hebrews 2:15). The primary purpose of the coming of the *Promised One* has to do with restoring mankind's ability to glorify God through the regeneration of lost souls "by grace through faith" and for humans to enjoy fellowship with God. This is God's "eternal purpose" in "the regeneration."

Satan does not want this "eternal purpose" to be accomplished. He opposes the restoration of dominion to humanity "in Christ." Therefore, *Antichristism* (as a movement) is anything that opposes the divine order of God by seeking to distort the glory (image) of God in which man was created, pervert the Word of God revealing God in all His attributes in glory, or anyone that lives contrary to the commands of God. False doctrine contributes to Satan's goal.

The *Antichrist* has always been the same individual since the fall of Satan. He has been the leader of the *Antichrist* movement throughout history. Antichristism is the ongoing lineage of the *seed of the serpent* down through the Dispensations (*Ages* or historical paradigms) of time. This *seed of the serpent* (manifested in the lives of unbelievers) opposes the stewardship and preservation of Truth by the remnant of God's chosen faithful.

What this all means to us is that there were (and are) no surprises to God. When Lucifer willfully rebelled against God's sovereignty in gifting dominion (*Federal Headship*) of His Genesis to Adam (and humanity in Adam), God was not surprised. God was not surprised by Eve's deception or Adam's willful, selfish choice to follow his wife's leadership rather than God's command. In other words, we do not find God looking over the catastrophe of His fallen creation and saying, "Oh, I never anticipated that happening!" God foreknew these events "before the foundation of the world" and instituted a plan for the recovery of every lost soul that would ever be procreated through God's planned continuum to populate the Earth. When Satan stole sovereignty over creation from Adam, he did not steal sovereignty from God. **By the very nature of God's condemnation, it reveals God's retention of His sovereignty.**

From before the beginning ("from the foundation of the world," Hebrews 4:3), God planned for a *New Genesis* with a new *Federal Head.* The *New Genesis* is what the Scriptures refer to as "the regeneration." This *New Genesis* is "in Christ," the *Promised One* referred to as "the Lamb slain from the foundation of the world."

The reason it is so important to understand that this *New Genesis* was already in place in God's plan prior to the details of the original *Genesis* of Genesis chapters one and two has to do with God's sovereignty over His creation and the issue of *primogeniture.* *Primogeniture* means the state of being the firstborn child with the right of succession belonging to the firstborn child, by which the whole real estate of an intestate passed to the eldest son.

The original *Genesis* was doomed to condemnation and destruction in the plan of God "before the foundation of the world." God foreknew this. The *New Genesis* is not a restoration of the fallen *Genesis*. The original, and now fallen *Genesis,* will be destroyed.

"⁹ The Lord is not slack concerning his promise, as some men count slackness; but is longsuffering to us-ward, not willing that any should perish, but that all should come to repentance. ¹⁰ But the day of the Lord will come as a thief in the night; in the which **the heavens shall pass away with a great noise, and the elements shall melt with fervent heat, the earth also** and the works that are therein shall be burned up. ¹¹ *Seeing* **then** *that* **all these things shall be dissolved**, what manner *of persons* ought ye to be in *all* holy conversation and godliness, ¹² Looking for and hasting unto the coming of the day of God, **wherein the heavens being on fire** shall be dissolved, and the elements shall melt with fervent heat?** [13] Nevertheless **we, according to his promise, look for new heavens and a new earth,** wherein dwelleth righteousness" (II Peter 3:9-13).

The *New Genesis* will be a completely new Creation. This *New Genesis* begins with the plan of God in the eternal Son of God becoming a man. Jesus is the *Promised One* of Genesis 3:15 and the Federal Head of the New Genesis, having already won victory over Satan's stolen dominion of the original creation when He died on Calvary and rose victorious over death. Jesus is the "firstborn" into the New Genesis through His resurrection and glorification, whereby through His death and resurrection He was "the firstborn among many brethren" (Romans 8:29) and "who is the beginning, the firstborn from the dead" (Colossians 1:15-18). **All those saved "by grace through faith" down through the Ages are God's *ultimate elect remnant*. They were not individuals chosen by God to be saved. These are individuals who chose to believe God and were saved.**

The Poisoned Tulip

Chapter Two
The Corporate/Vocational View of Election
Corporately and Vocationally Elect "in Christ"

Why is the title of this book *The Poisoned TULIP*? The Acronym TULIP does not actually come from Calvin or Augustine. The TULIP acronym comes from the Dutch Reformed church and the Synod of Dort (1618– 1619) led by Theodore Beza and other Calvinists. The Synod of Dort listed what came to be called "the five heads of Dort" in the acronym TULIP. Of course, the nation of the Dutch people is Holland, which is the *land of the tulip*. There is little wonder why the synod of Dort chose the tulip to represent their acronym. However, they did not think through the association of their acronym with the tulip in general. Although the tulip has a beautiful flower, everything except the petals of the flower is poison to ingest. This is equally true of TULIP theology. It is *theological poison*.

The whole doctrine of election is found "in Christ" as the "door" to "the regeneration" (Ephesians 1:1). **Jesus Christ, the God/man, is the foundation of the doctrine of election.** This goes beyond the propitiation of God's wrath and the justification of sinners "by grace through faith." This goes beyond the means ("by grace") and the method ("through faith"). **These aspects of Christ's redemptive work open a "door" of salvation into "the regeneration" (*New Genesis*) "in Christ."** Being "born again" out from the condemned Adamic creation is not the end of the New Covenant "in Christ." This is merely the beginning of "our so great salvation." Being "born again" is a removal from one existence (the "darkness" of the Adamic curse) and an entrance into a new existence (the "light" of the *New Genesis*). **Throughout the Ages, Jesus (the *Promised One*) has been the promised "door" into the *New Genesis*.**

"In Christ" is Biblical terminology meaning being "born again" into "the regeneration" (*New Genesis*) "by grace" and "through faith" (Ephesians 2:8-9) with Jesus being the new Federal Head ("last Adam," I Corinthians 15:45) of this *New Genesis*. All those who are "born again" are corporately and vocationally elect to engage the forces of evil and darkness and to become "workers together with God" (II Corinthians 6:1) to bring "many sons unto glory" (Hebrews 2:10).

"[1] Verily, verily, I say unto you, He that **entereth not by the door into the sheepfold**, but climbeth up some other way, the same is a thief and a robber. [2] But **he that entereth in by the door is the shepherd of the sheep**. [3] To him the porter openeth; and the sheep hear his voice: and he calleth his own sheep by name, and leadeth them out. [4] And when he putteth forth his own sheep, **he goeth before them**, and the sheep follow him: for they know his voice. [5] And a stranger will they not follow, but will flee from him: for they know not the voice of strangers. [6] This parable spake Jesus unto them: but they understood not what things they were which he spake unto them. [7] Then said Jesus unto them again, Verily, verily, I say unto you, **I am the door of the sheep**. [8] All that ever came before me are thieves and robbers: but the sheep did not hear them. [9] **I am the door: by me if any man enter in, he shall be saved, and shall go in and out, and find pasture.** [10] The thief cometh not, but for to steal, and to kill, and to destroy: **I am come that they might have life, and that they might have *it* more abundantly. [11] I am the good shepherd: the good shepherd giveth his life for the sheep.** [12] But he that is an hireling, and not the shepherd, whose own the sheep are not, seeth the wolf coming, and leaveth the sheep, and fleeth: and the wolf catcheth them, and scattereth the sheep. [13] The hireling fleeth, because he is an hireling, and careth not for the sheep. **[14] I am the good shepherd, and know my *sheep*, and am known of mine. [15] As the Father knoweth me, even so know I the Father: and I lay down my life for the sheep.** [16] And other sheep I have, which are not of this fold: them also I must bring, and they shall hear my voice; and **there shall be one fold, *and* one shepherd**" (John 10:1-16).

John 10:1-6 is a critical text to understanding the doctrine of election. It cannot be understood apart from its historical context. Here, the historical context is critical to "rightly dividing the Word of truth." The text lies within a period of historical transitioning from the Dispensation of Law to the Dispensation of Grace.

At the time of Christ's arrival upon the scene of history and the beginning of His ministry at the age of thirty, the nation of Israel had been led into apostasy by the apostate priesthood of Israel (the "scribes and Pharisees," Matthew 23:13-32). Yet, there were many individuals within the nation of Israel that were saved "by grace through faith." These *saved* Jews comprised the group that Christ refers to as the "sheepfold," referring to *spiritual* Israel or "the regeneration" (those trusting in the Promised One; Romans 9:8 and Galatians 3:6-16; although only *positionally* regenerated and justified at this point in history of the writing of the Gospel of John in that they had not yet received the indwelling of the Spirit, John 14:17).

There were also lost Jews within the nation of Israel that thought they were within the "sheepfold" due to their seminal connection to Abraham (Romans 9:7). They had not entered "by the door *{faith in Christ alone for the gift of justification}* into the sheepfold." In other words, they were not part of "the regeneration" or the "sheepfold." These national Jews sought entrance to the "sheepfold" through the *door* of seminal connection to Abraham and "the works of the Law. This is what the apostate religious leaders of Israel were teaching. These are the individuals Christ refers to by the words "climbeth up some other way" (John 10:1). The only "door" that could truly bring the sinner into the "sheepfold" of "the regeneration" was faith in the "door," which is Jesus the *Promised One.* **Faith was a choice, even though these Jews were elect nationally.**

We tend to see the "sheepfold" through the eyes of modern examples. We think of a "sheepfold" as an area surrounded by a fenced area separated by some distance from the shepherd's living quarters. The word "sheepfold" at the time of Christ referred to a courtyard surrounded by a wall and often directly connected to the living quarters.

Away from a city or a residence, the "sheepfold" was often a cave or recessed area on a hillside. The shepherd would sleep in the opening to guard the sheep inside. He became the *door of entrance* into the sheepfold. This is where the sheep were brought for the night. This would parallel to what Christ refers in John chapter fourteen. The "sheepfold" does not refer to *national* Israel. The "sheepfold" refers to *spiritual* Israel (i.e., saved Jews) that were positionally regenerated "by grace through faith" in the *Promised One,* even though national Israel was corporately elect.

"[1] Let not your heart be troubled: ye believe in God, believe also in me. [2] **In my Father's house are many mansions**: if *it were* not *so*, I would have told you. **I go to prepare a place for you.** [3] And if I go and prepare a place for you, I will come again, and receive you unto myself; that **where I am,** *there* **ye may be also**" (John 14:1-3).

The **"shepherd" would need to enter the "sheepfold" ("the regeneration") in the same way as the** *sheep.* **He would need to die, be resurrected, and be glorified to become the New Federal Head of "the regeneration" (the** *New Genesis***).**

> "And Jesus said unto them, Verily I say unto you, That ye **which have followed me** {*akolouthéō; to be in the same way with; i.e., glorification*}, **in the regeneration** {*the New Creation*} when the Son of man shall sit in the throne of his glory, **ye** {*the twelve apostles*} also shall sit upon twelve thrones, judging the twelve tribes of Israel" (Matthew 19:28).

Therefore, Jesus' human death, burial, resurrection, and glorification made Him the "firstborn" from the dead into "the regeneration." Since Jesus was without sin, His death was vicariously offered to propitiate God's wrath upon sin, opening the "door" to "whosoever will" to enter "the regeneration" "by grace through faith" in Christ's "finished" work of redemption and reconciliation. Therefore, Christ becomes both the *shepherd* and the "door" into the "sheepfold" ("the regeneration").

Christ is the "firstborn" of "the regeneration" and its new *Federal Head.* God's *foreknowledge* regarding election is the *foreknowledge* of all those throughout the Ages that would trust in the *Promised One* of Genesis 3:15. Jesus was born into humanity to *crush* the "head" (*Federal Headship*) of Satan taken from Adam through Eve's deception. These believers are the "other sheep" referred to in John 10:16. There were saved people prior to the Abrahamic Covenant and the establishment of the nation of Israel and there would be saved Gentiles in the Church Age that would be "born again" into "the regeneration."

Church Age believers (saved Jews and saved Gentiles will be the new Priesthood of Israel during the Kingdom Age) will be the "kings" of which Jesus will be "King" and they will be the "lords" of which Jesus will be "Lord" (Revelation 17:14). These Church Age believers will rule with Jesus in glorified bodies over the restored Kingdom of Israel (a one world Theocracy) (Revelation 2:27; 3:21).

"*4* To whom {*Jesus Christ*} coming, *as unto* a living stone, disallowed indeed of men, but **chosen of God**, *and* precious, *5* Ye also {*Church Age believers*}, as lively stones, are built up a spiritual house, an holy priesthood, to offer up spiritual sacrifices, acceptable to God by Jesus Christ. *6* Wherefore also it is contained in the scripture, Behold, I lay in Sion a chief corner stone {*Jesus Christ*}, **elect, precious**: and he that believeth on him shall not be confounded. *7* Unto you therefore which believe *he is* precious: but unto them which be disobedient {*the rejected Aaronic Priesthood of National Israel*}, the stone which the builders disallowed, the same is made the head of the corner, *8* And a stone of stumbling, and a rock of offence, *even to them* which stumble at the word, being disobedient: whereunto also they were appointed. *9* But ye {*Church Age believers*} *are* **a chosen generation**, a **royal priesthood**, an **holy nation**, a peculiar people; that **ye should shew forth the praises of him who hath called you out of darkness into his marvellous light**: *10* Which in time past *were* not a people, but *are* now the people of God: which had not obtained mercy, but now have obtained mercy" (I Peter 2:4-10).

The objective facts of Christ's death, burial, resurrection, and glorification are the "corner" stone of

"the regeneration." Apart from this living "corner stone" the edifice of a living Temple of "lively stones" to the glory of God could not be constructed. The reference to Christ as the Elect "living stone" and to all believers "as lively stones" is to the *Temple* that God has created to His glory, first in "the Church" (i.e., "body" of Christ) and, ultimately in "the regeneration" (i.e., "new creation"). **This living *Temple* will be the corporate unification of all believers into a living organism of eternal worship and praise to God.**

"[1] For we know that **if our earthly house** {*the human body is mere clothing for the soul/spirit*} of *this* tabernacle were dissolved, we have a building of God, **an house not made with hands, eternal in the heavens**. [2] For in this we groan, earnestly desiring to be clothed upon **with our house which is from heaven** {*glorification*}: [3] If so be that being clothed we shall not be found naked. [4] For we that are in *this* tabernacle do groan, being burdened: not for that we would be unclothed, but clothed upon, that mortality might be swallowed up of life. [5] Now he that hath wrought us for the selfsame thing *is* God, who also hath given unto us the earnest of the Spirit" (II Corinthians 5:1-5).

Is Corporate and Vocational Election a New Doctrine?

Numerous respectable Bible scholars have taught corporate and vocational election for many centuries. We must remember that the doctrine of *Sovereign Grace* (salvational election and Monergism) was not really systematized until John Calvin's *Institutes of Religion*, first edition published in A.D. 1536 in Basel, Switzerland. The *Institutes of Religion* was simply a restatement and elaboration of Augustine's theology (Roman Catholicism). However, there were numerous oppositions to Calvin's

Calvinism from the time it was originally published. However, most of the classically trained theologians of the period were using the same *deductive hermeneutical methodology* as Calvin. Few, if any, were using an *inductive hermeneutical methodology.*

> ". . . The term *inductive* is used in both a broader and narrower sense. In the broader sense, it involves a commitment to move from the evidence of the text and the realities that surround the text to possible conclusions (or inferences) regarding the meaning of the text. In this sense, *inductive* is practically synonymous with *evidential* over against *deductive*, which is presuppositional, involving a movement from presuppositions with which one approaches the text to a reading of the text intended to support these presuppositions."[7]

The *inductive hermeneutical methodology* (grammar of text + historical context = conclusion or meaning) was common until Augustine introduced *Aristotelian Syllogism* into interpretation of the Bible. In simplest terms *Aristotelian Syllogism* is *deductive logic* which posits a *major premise* plus a *minor premise,* reaching a *conclusion* from the composite logic between the two premises. For instance, the Jehovah Witnesses use *Aristotelian Syllogism* and deductive logic to prove Jesus is not God. Their *major premise* is that God is eternal. Their *minor premise* is that Jesus had a beginning. Their *conclusion* then is that Jesus cannot be God because Jesus has a beginning.

---

[7] David R. Bauer and Robert A. Traina, *Inductive Bible Study: A Comprehensive Guide to the Practice of Hermeneutics,* Baker Academic a division of Baker Publishing Group, Grand Rapids, MI.

Of course, the failure in the *minor premise* is that Jesus' beginning is when Jehovah became incarnate in a human body. Therefore, Jesus is BOTH God and man. It becomes apparent in this instance how faulty *Aristotelian Syllogism* and *deductive logic* can be. They become faulty when one of the *premises* upon which the *conclusion* is reached is faulty or a *presupposition* without any Scriptural foundation. If the goal is to disprove the deity of Christ, such a goal is easily accomplished through *Aristotelian Syllogism* and *deductive logic.* However, that goal becomes impossible when confronted with an *inductive hermeneutical methodology.*

Numerous well-known theologians have used *inductive hermeneutical methodology* to establish that election in the Bible is *primarily* corporate and vocational. I say *primarily* because there are occasions when individuals were elected for a specific purpose also. J. B. Lightfoot (A.D. 1828-1889) addresses corporate election in his **Notes on the Epistles of St. Paul**[8] regarding Ephesians 1:4 (page 312) as quoted in Robert Shank's (A.D. 1918-2006) book, ***Elect in the Son.***[9]

"*en Christo*] i.e. 'by virtue of our incorporation in, our union with, Christ.' As God seated us in heaven 'in Christ' (ii. 6), so also His blessings upon us there in Him.

en auto] i.e. en Christo. In God's eternal purpose the believers are contemplated as existing in Christ, as the Head, the Summary, of the race. The *ekloge* [the election] has no separate existence independently of the

---

[8] J.B. Lightfoot, *Notes on the Epistles of St. Paul*, page 312.
[9] Robert Shank, *Elect in the Son*, Bethany House Publishers, Minneapolis, Minn., page 43.

eklektos (Luke ix.35, xxiii.35) [the chosen One, Christ]. The election of Christ involves implicitly the election of the Church."

Lightfoot's statement, "the election of Christ involves implicitly the election of the Church," is a clear representation of the central idea communicated in Ephesians 1:3-14. Election is *corporate*. The words "chosen us in Him" clearly refers to the corporate entity of the Church as a unity. This union is of all believers "in Christ" and is what the context of the epistle to the Ephesians is about, i.e., the election of all Church Age believers corporately and vocationally as a new priesthood.

John Peter Lange (A.D. 1802-1884), a Calvinist theologian, in his ***Commentary on the Holy Scriptures: Ephesians*** says:

" . . . 'us' should be taken in its wider meaning . . . and should not be limited to the Apostle . . . nor to the Jewish Christians, but applies to His people, all men, who have become or will become Christians."[10]

Lange makes a similar comment regarding Romans 8:28-30 in his ***Commentary on the Holy Scriptures: Romans***:

" . . . Christ is the elect in God's real kingdom in the absolute sense, so that all His followers are chosen with Him as organic members, according to their organic relations (Eph.i)."[11]

---

[10] John Peter Lange, *Commentary on the Holy Scriptures: Ephesians*, page 28 as quoted by Robert Shank in *Elect in the Son*, page 45.

[11] John Peter Lange, *Commentary on the Holy Scriptures: Romans*, page 290 as quoted by Robert Shank in *Elect in the Son*, page 45.

Dr. M. G. Cambron (A.D. 1911-2000) in his book *The New Testament, A Book-by-Book Survey* (pages 201, 203) states:

"The words chosen and election have to do with the purpose of God in service. Israel was that chosen nation which God used to preach the Kingdom of God to the world. The Church is that nation through whom God is now preaching the Kingdom of God. The only requisite to become the called of God is faith."[12]

This corporate entity called the Church, and the "body" of Christ is the "tabernacle, not made with hands" referred to in Hebrews 9:11. It is also what is being referred to in Colossians 1:18 (Christ, the "head of the body, the church: who is the beginning, the firstborn from the dead") and Hebrews 12:23 (the "general assembly and church of the firstborn").

"[8] The Holy Ghost this signifying, that the way into the holiest of all {*the heavenly Holy of Holies and the Throne of Grace*} was not yet made manifest, while as the first tabernacle {*Mosaic Covenant Temple*} was yet standing: [9] Which *was* a figure for the time then present, in which were offered both gifts and sacrifices, **that could not make him that did the service perfect**, as pertaining to the conscience; [10] *Which stood* only in meats and drinks, and divers washings, and carnal ordinances, imposed *on them* until the time of reformation. [11] But Christ **being come an high priest** of good things to come, **by a greater and more perfect**

---

[12] Cameron, Mark G., *The New Testament: a Book By Book Survey*, Zondervan Publishing House, Grand Rapids, MI, January 1, 1995.

tabernacle, not made with hands, that is to say, not of this building; [12] Neither by the blood of goats and calves, but by his own blood **he entered in once into the holy place, having obtained eternal redemption *for us*.** [13] For if the blood of bulls and of goats, and the ashes of an heifer sprinkling the unclean, sanctifieth to the purifying of the flesh: [14] How much more shall the blood of Christ, who through the eternal Spirit offered himself without spot to God, purge your conscience from dead works to serve the living God? [15] And for this cause he is the mediator of the new testament, that by means of death, for the redemption of the transgressions *that were* under the first testament, they which are called might receive **the promise of eternal inheritance**" (Hebrews 9:8-15).

"[10] For it became him {*Jesus Christ*}, for whom *are* all things, and by whom *are* all things, in **bringing many sons unto glory**, to make the captain of their salvation perfect through sufferings. [11] For both he that sanctifieth and they who are sanctified *are* **all of one**: for which cause he is not ashamed to call them brethren, [12] Saying, I will declare thy name unto my brethren, in the midst of the church will I sing praise unto thee. [13] And again, I will put my trust in him. And again, Behold I and the children which God hath given me. [14] **Forasmuch then as the children are partakers of flesh and blood, he also himself likewise took part of the same; that through death he might destroy him that had the power of death, that is, the devil;** [15] And deliver them who through fear of death were all their lifetime subject to bondage. [16] For verily he took not on *him the nature of* angels; but **he took on *him* the seed of Abraham**" (Hebrews 2:10-16).

Many well-known scholars see election as vocational and corporate in the epistle to the Ephesians. **Ephesians 1:3-14 is a classic text on election. Yet it is one of the most misinterpreted texts in the Bible.** It is misinterpreted because the presuppositions of Calvinism/Arminianism are imposed upon the text. The first supposition is that election refers to God choosing certain individuals to be saved from condemnation to Hell. Robert Shank in his book *Elect in The Son* (Bethany House Publishers) says:

"The paramount importance of the passage rests in the fact that it contains the Bible's most definitive statement of a profound doctrine of the Holy Scriptures: God's gracious election of men **in Christ** before the foundation of the world and the **predestination of the elect** to holy privilege and everlasting felicity. **Of all passages of Scripture touching the matter of election, Ephesians 1:3-14 is the foundation passage.** Referring to Ephesians 1:4, 9 and the cognate verse II Timothy 1:9, G.C. Berkouwer observes that "the history of the doctrine of election may be interpreted as an effort to understand the meaning of these words[13]." (bolding added)

Shank then goes on to quote Berkouwer, "There is election only in Christ . . . God's election is election in Christ."[14] Election *in Christ* is clearly the emphasis of the text as shown by the phrases "in Christ" (vs. 3 and 10),

---

[13] Shank makes the notation in a footnote: "G.C. Berkouwer, *Divine Election*, p. 135. Professor of Systematic Theology at Free University of Amsterdam, Berkouwer is among the foremost Calvinist theologians of today and representative of the Reformed tradition."
[14] Ibid, pp. 149,162.

"chosen us in him" (vs. 4), "accepted in the beloved" (vs. 6), "purposed in himself" (vs. 9) and "in whom" (vs. 11 and 13).

The question we must ask and answer to understand this text's teaching on election is: **What does the phrase "in Christ" mean as it relates to what God is saying about election?** Of course, the answer is to allow Scripture to interpret Scripture (*Sola Scriptura*). There are many Scriptures that use the phrase "in Christ." For brevity, I will refer only to the most definitive of these texts.

> "[12] For as the body is one, and hath many members, and all the members of that one body, being many, are one body: so also *is* Christ. [13] For by one Spirit are we all {*Spirit*} **baptized into one body**, whether *we be* Jews or Gentiles, whether *we be* bond or free; and have been all made to drink into one Spirit. [14] For the body is not one member, but many" (I Corinthians 12:12-14).

The "one body" into which all believers are "baptized" "by" the "Spirit" is the *body* of Christ ("the regeneration," Matthew 19:28). The *body* of Christ refers initially to the "church of the firstborn" (Hebrews 12:23), but ultimately to "the regeneration" under the new *Federal Headship* of Jesus Christ. This becomes apparent as we look at the use of the phrase "in Christ" inductively throughout its New Testament usage. This will also define the doctrine of election "in Christ" as referred to in Ephesians 1:3-14. **The words "in Christ" and "in Adam" are critical phrases to understanding the doctrine of election.**

> "[12] Now if Christ be preached that he rose from the dead, how say some among you that there is no resurrection of the dead? [13] But if there be no resurrection of the dead, then is Christ not risen: [14] And if Christ be not risen, then *is* our preaching vain, and your faith *is* also

vain. [15] Yea, and we are found false witnesses of God; because we have testified of God that he raised up Christ: whom he raised not up, if so be that the dead rise not. [16] For if the dead rise not, then is not Christ raised: [17] And if Christ be not raised, your faith *is* vain; ye are yet in your sins. [18] Then they also which are fallen asleep **in Christ** are perished. [19] If in this life only we have hope **in Christ**, we are of all men most miserable. [20] But now is Christ risen from the dead, *and* become **the firstfruits** of them that slept. [21] For since by man *came* death, by man *came* also the resurrection of the dead. [22] For as **in Adam all die**, even so **in Christ shall all be made alive**. [23] But every man in his own order: **Christ the firstfruits**; afterward they that are Christ's at his coming. [24] Then *cometh* the end, when he shall have delivered up the kingdom to God, even the Father; when he shall have put down all rule and all authority and power. [25] **For he must reign, till he hath put all enemies under his feet.** [26] The last enemy *that* shall be destroyed *is* death. [27] For he hath put all things under his feet. But when he saith all things are put under *him, it is* manifest that he is excepted, which did put all things under him. [28] And when all things shall be subdued unto him, then shall the Son also himself be subject unto him that put all things under him, that God may be all in all" (I Corinthians 15:12-28).

    As we saw earlier in John chapter ten, Christ is both the Shepherd of the sheep and the "door" into the "sheepfold." The "porter" in that text (John 10:3) is the Person of the Holy Spirit. People are "born again" into the "sheepfold." The "sheepfold" is "the regeneration" ("in Christ" equals "new creature;" literally *"new creation,"* II Corinthians 5:17). **The fact that Christ is "risen from the dead" and glorified is critical to His transition into "the**

regeneration." He opens the "door" (*which 'door' is Himself as the Last Adam*) into "the regeneration" for "whosoever will" by His universal propitiation (I John 2:2) of God's wrath (condemnation).

As a glorified human, Jesus passes into "the regeneration" as its *Federal Head* in His resurrection and glorification. Christ's act of the propitiation of God's wrath through His substitutionary death leaves the "door" into "the regeneration" open to anyone willing to believe the objective facts of the Gospel and confess Jesus as Lord, calling on Him to save/rescue him from the fallen creation and its condemnation (Romans 10:9-13). This is the meaning of Christ being the "door" into the "Sheepfold." He as well *leads* His "sheep," through His personal glorification and ascension to the Father, into the "Sheepfold" (Ephesians 4:8) "by grace through faith" (Ephesians 2:8).

"[16] Wherefore henceforth know we no man after the flesh: yea, though we have known Christ after the flesh, yet now henceforth know we *him* no more. [17] Therefore if any man *be* **in Christ**, *he is* a new creature: old things are passed away; behold, all things are become new. [18] And all things *are* of God, who hath reconciled us to himself by Jesus Christ, and hath given to us the ministry of reconciliation; [19] To wit, that God was **in Christ**, reconciling the world unto himself, not imputing their trespasses unto them; and hath committed unto us the word of reconciliation. [20] Now then we are ambassadors for Christ, as though God did beseech *you* by us: we pray *you* in Christ's stead, be ye reconciled to God. [21] For he hath made him *to be* sin for us, who knew no sin; that we might be made the righteousness of God **in him**" (II Corinthians 5:16-21).

The fact that believers are Spirit baptized into the "body" of Christ at the moment of their salvation is an evident reality. "Therefore, if any man *be* in Christ, *he is a new creature: old things are passed away; behold, all things are become new" (II Corinthians 5:17). Being "in Christ" means that believer has become, by a divine act of regeneration, "a new creature." The "old things" (all aspects of the believer's old life in the fallen creation and "in Adam") have "passed away" positionally once for all when the believer is baptized "in Christ." God has chosen (elected) the Shepherd (Christ) and the "sheepfold" ("the regeneration" or "new creation"). **"Whosoever" can become part of that election by entering the "sheepfold" through the "door" of faith in Christ (the Shepherd).**

"[26] For **ye are all** {*Jews and Gentiles alike*} the children of God by faith in Christ Jesus. [27] For as many of you as have been {*Spirit*} baptized **into Christ** have put on Christ. [28] There is neither Jew nor Greek, there is neither bond nor free, there is neither male nor female: for ye are all **one in Christ** Jesus {*see Ephesians 4:1-6*}. [29] And if ye *be* Christ's, then are ye Abraham's seed {*see Galatians 3:16*}, and heirs {*see Ephesians 1:11, 14, 18 and I Peter 1:4*} according to the promise {*i.e., Abrahamic Covenant*}" (Galatians 3:26-29).

"For **in Christ** Jesus neither circumcision availeth any thing, nor uncircumcision, but a new creature" (Galatians 6:15).

"In Christ" "neither circumcision" (being a Jew) has any merit, "nor uncircumcision" (being a Gentile) has any merit. The only thing that matters, or has any merit, is to become "a new creature" (i.e., one of "the regeneration"). A place in, and being part of, "the regeneration" is the believer's inheritance. Regenerated believers are Christ's "inheritance" in "the regeneration." This "mighty power" of regeneration was "wrought in Christ, when He {*God*} raised him from the dead" (see Ephesians 1:15-23 below). **Election is "in Christ." If a person is "in Christ," He BECOMES one of the elect.**

"[15] Wherefore I also, after I heard of your faith in the Lord Jesus, and love unto all the saints, [16] Cease not to give thanks for you, making mention of you in my prayers; [17] That the God of our Lord Jesus Christ, **the Father of glory, may give unto you** {*in illumination*} the spirit of wisdom and revelation in the knowledge of him: [18] The **eyes of your understanding being enlightened**; that ye may know what **is the hope of his calling** {*vocationally*} , and **what the riches of the glory of his inheritance in the saints,** [19] And what *is* the exceeding greatness of his power to us-ward **who believe**, according to the working of his mighty power, [20] Which he wrought **in Christ**, when he raised him from the dead, and **set *him* at his own right hand** {*new federal headship of Christ*} in the heavenly *places,* [21] Far above all principality, and power, and might, and dominion, and every name that is named, **not only in this world, but also in that which is to come** {*the New Creation*}: [22] And hath put all *things* under his feet, and gave him *to be* **the head over all *things* to the church** {*the new priesthood of all believers*}, [23] Which is his body, the fulness of him that filleth all in all" (Ephesians 1:15-23).

"[6] And hath **raised *us* up together** {*aorist, i.e., an event = position 'in Christ'*}, and made *us* sit together {*aorist, i.e., an event = position 'in Christ'*} in heavenly *places* **in Christ Jesus:** [7] That in **the ages to come** {*Kingdom*

Age rule with Christ} he might shew the exceeding riches of his grace in *his* kindness toward us **through Christ Jesus.** [8] For **by grace are ye saved** {*perfect, passive*} through faith; and that not of yourselves: ***it is*** {*salvation*} the gift of God: [9] Not of works, lest any man should boast. [10] For **we are his workmanship** {*thing made or created*}, **created** {*aorist, i.e., an event = position 'in Christ'*}, **in Christ Jesus** unto good works, which God hath before ordained that we should walk in them. [11] Wherefore remember, that ye *being* in time past Gentiles in the flesh, who are called Uncircumcision by that which is called the Circumcision in the flesh made by hands; [12] That at that time ye were without Christ, being aliens from the commonwealth of Israel, and strangers from the covenants of promise, having no hope, and without God in the world: [13] But now **in Christ Jesus** ye who sometimes were far off are made nigh by the blood of Christ. [14] For he is our peace, who hath made **both one**, and hath broken down the middle wall of partition *between us*; [15] Having abolished in his flesh the enmity, *even* the law of commandments *contained* in ordinances; for to make **in himself** of twain one new man, *so* making peace; [16] And that he might reconcile both unto God **in one body** by the cross, having slain the enmity thereby: [17] And came and preached peace to you which were afar off, and to them that were nigh. [18] For through him we both have access by one Spirit unto the Father. [19] Now therefore ye are no more strangers and foreigners, but **fellowcitizens with the saints, and of the household of God**; [20] And are built upon the foundation of the apostles and prophets, **Jesus Christ himself being the chief corner *stone*;** [21] **In whom** all the building fitly framed together **groweth unto an holy temple in the Lord** {*the New Heaven/Earth*}: [22] **In whom** ye also are builded together for an habitation of God through the Spirit" (Ephesians 2:6-22).

"[13] But I would not have you to be ignorant, brethren, concerning them which are asleep, that ye sorrow not, even as others which have no hope. [14] For if we believe that Jesus died and rose again, even so them also which **sleep in Jesus** will God bring with him. [15] For this we say unto you by the word of the Lord, that we which are alive *and* remain unto the coming of the Lord shall not prevent them which are asleep. [16] For the Lord himself shall descend from heaven with a shout, with the voice of the archangel, and with the trump of God: and the **dead in Christ** shall rise first: [17] Then we which are alive *and* remain shall be caught up together with them in the clouds, to meet the Lord in the air: and so shall we ever be with the Lord. [18] Wherefore comfort one another with these words" (I Thessalonians 4:13-18).

Isaiah 49:1-12 certainly reveals that Christ is the prophesized Deliverer. However, the emphasis of deliverance is often focused more on what the sinner is delivered *from* rather than where/what the believer is delivered *to*. **From what the sinner is delivered is secondary *to* what the believer is delivered.** The sinner is delivered *from* God's wrath in His condemnation of the first creation and the Adamic race. The believer is delivered *into* God's grace (Romans 5:2) and the unfolding of "the regeneration" eschatologically.

"[1] Listen, O isles, unto me {*the Son of God*}; and hearken, ye people, from far; The LORD hath called me from the womb {*of creation; Revelation 13:8*}; from the bowels of my mother hath he made mention of my name. [2] And he hath made my mouth like a sharp sword;

in the shadow of his hand hath he hid me {*the mystery of Christ and "the regeneration"*}, and made me a polished shaft; in his quiver hath he hid me; [3] And said unto me, Thou *art* my servant, O Israel, in whom I will be glorified {*revealed in all of His majestic attributes*}. [4] Then I said, I have laboured in vain, I have spent my strength for nought, and in vain: *yet* surely my judgment *is* with the LORD, and my work with my God {*propitiation*}. [5] And now, saith the LORD that formed me from the womb *to be* his servant, to bring Jacob again to him, Though Israel be not gathered, yet shall I be glorious in the eyes of the LORD, and my God shall be my strength. [6] And he said, It is a light thing that thou shouldest be my servant to raise up the tribes of Jacob, and to restore the preserved of Israel: I will also give thee for a light to the Gentiles, that thou mayest be my salvation unto the end of the earth {*whosoever*}. [7] Thus saith the LORD, the Redeemer of Israel, *and* his Holy One, to him whom man despiseth, to him whom the nation abhorreth, to a servant of rulers, Kings shall see and arise, princes also shall worship, because of the LORD that is faithful, *and* the Holy One of Israel, and he shall choose thee. [8] Thus saith the LORD, In an acceptable time have I heard thee, and in a day of salvation {*Galatians 4:4*} have I helped thee: and I will preserve thee, and give thee for a covenant of the people, to establish the earth, to cause to inherit the desolate heritages; [9] That thou mayest say to the prisoners, Go forth; to them that *are* in darkness, Shew yourselves. They shall feed in the ways, and their pastures *shall be* in all high places. [10] They shall not hunger nor thirst; neither shall the heat nor sun smite them: for he that hath mercy on them shall lead them, even by the springs of water shall he guide them. [11] And I will make all my mountains a way, and my highways shall be exalted" (Isaiah 49:1-12).

Isaiah 49:9-12 literates the idea of John 10: 1-16 in the restoration of the nation of Israel during the Kingdom Age and the Church Age saints as the "other sheep have I" of John 10:16. The Kingdom Age is only a partial fulfillment of Isaiah 49:9-12. This prophecy is not completely fulfilled until the creation of the New Heaven/Earth and the final phase of "the regeneration."

"Unlike Calvin's thesis that particular men are unconditionally elect from eternity and other particular men are unconditionally reprobate, the thesis that election to salvation is corporate and comprehends individuals only in identification and association with the elect body does not require for its defense ingenious interpretations of simple, explicit categorical statements of Scripture."[15]

---

[15] Robert Shank, *Elect In The Son*; Bethany House Publishers, Minneapolis, Minn., page 48.

The Poisoned Tulip

Chapter Three
The Corporate/Vocational View of Election
Is Calvinism's Total Depravity a Bible Doctrine

"Beloved, when I gave all diligence to write unto you of the common salvation, it was needful for me to write unto you, and exhort *you* that ye **should earnestly contend for <u>the</u> faith** which was once delivered unto the saints" (Jude 3).

The word *apologetics* is from a Greek word that means *to speak in defense. Apologetics* is the religious discipline of defending right doctrine primarily through hermeneutical and systematic presentation of truth through conversational or written discourse. **Hermeneutics is teaching people how to feed themselves Biblically and spiritually.**

However, Biblical *apologetics* is forced to address *logical arguments* as well as faulty and errant Biblical arguments to "earnestly contend for **the faith** which was **once delivered** *{aorist = an event that has happened}* **unto the saints** *{deposited into their guardianship for defending right doctrine}*" (Jude 3). **Defending right doctrine against Calvinism includes the necessary *apologetics* that addresses both faulty and errant Biblical arguments intermixed with a hermeneutic of presuppositions based upon logical arguments as opposed to Biblical hermeneutical arguments.** Calvinism comes to the arena of *apologetics* disguised as Biblical, hiding behind *Aristotelian Syllogism* or deductive logic disguised as Biblical hermeneutics.

Biblicists that allow this *apologetic* discourse to go on without addressing the hermeneutical corruption of *Sola Scriptura* by allowing *Aristotelian Syllogism* to introduce eisegetical presuppositions into the discourse will find themselves involved in foolish *intellectualism.* This foolish *intellectualism* will generate forced *logical deductions* based on proof texts into which Calvinism's presupposition are read and imposed. The five statements of the TULIP acronym lack any real exegetical support except through proof texting of their eisegetical presuppositions.

Exegesis = out from the Bible
Eisegesis = into the Bible

The person seeking to address and expose the faulty and corrupted eisegetical presuppositions of Calvinism's hermeneutics is forced to use, define, and explain terms often only used by theological professionals. In using, defining, and explaining these terms those doing so are forced to enter the arena of the *pseudo-intellectualism* that is really a *hallmark characteristic* of Calvinism. Anyone challenging the presuppositional statements of the TULIP acronym is simply dismissed as lacking the intellectual acumen to understand Calvinism.

Therefore, Calvinists simply dismiss anyone disagreeing with them as merely *ignorant schoolboys* who do not even deserve a hearing. Calvinists refuse to surrender the *pseudo-high ground* gained by their *pseudo-intellectualism* by dismissing anyone disagreeing with them as intellectual inferiors lacking the educational credentials to even enter the discourse.

Sovereignty, as it is used of God, is a *judicial term* and is not equal to *predeterminism/predestination* (fatalism). God's sovereignty does not mean He is the *cause of all things.* It simply means God is the final and ultimate authority in all things.

"Unlike Calvin's thesis that particular men are unconditionally elect from eternity and other particular men are unconditionally reprobate, the thesis that election to salvation is corporate and comprehends individuals only in identification and association with the elect body does not require for its defense ingenious interpretations of simple, explicit categorical statements of Scripture."[16]

Total depravity does not mean *total inability*.

There are numerous false teachings about the fall of humanity into sin. There is the false doctrine that all humans have Adam's sin imputed to them by God at either conception or birth. Calvinists go beyond the consequences of the fall of Adam whereby his nature was corrupted by his own choice, thereby seminally passing a sin nature to his progeny that is totally devoid of any possibility of perfect holiness before God. **The seminally inherent human sin nature corrupts in the human heart (emotions), mind (thinking and imaginations), and body (actions).**

"[12] Wherefore, as **by one man** sin entered into the world, and death by sin; and so death passed upon all men, for that all have sinned: [13] (For until the law sin was in the world: but **sin is not imputed when there is no law**. [14] Nevertheless **death reigned** from Adam to Moses, **even over them that had not sinned after the similitude of Adam's transgression**, who is the figure of him that was to come" (Romans 5:12-14).

Calvinists teach that humans inherit Adam's *guilt* for his original sin. They believe Adam's *guilt* is imputed to

---

[16] Robert Shank, *Elect In The Son*; Bethany House Publishers, Minneapolis, Minn., page 48.

all humans. If this is true, God holds people guilty for something someone else has done. **Is the son guilty for the father's sin?** God answers this question in Ezekiel chapter eighteen as God puts forth a scenario of a hypothetical father who lives righteously and selflessly (Ezekiel 18:1-10) and begets a son who is morally reprobate. Will the moral father be punished for what the immoral son does? Or vice versus, will the moral son be punished for what the immoral father does? If either of these scenarios were true about God, could God be considered fair or just in His judgments? **A son or father may take upon himself the shame of sin, but need never take upon himself the guilt.** God does not do so, and neither should the father/son or anyone else. **To purport anything else is serious error.**

"[19] Yet say ye, **Why? doth not the son bear the iniquity of the father?** When the son hath done that which is lawful and right, *and* hath kept all my statutes, and hath done them, he shall surely live. [20] The soul that sinneth, it shall die. **The son shall not bear the iniquity of the father, neither shall the father bear the iniquity of the son**: the righteousness of the righteous shall be upon him, and the wickedness of the wicked shall be upon him" (Ezekiel 18:19-20).

Calvinism's teaching of total depravity is Augustine's teaching restated. Augustine's (A.D. 354-430) teaching on total depravity was birthed out debate with Pelagius (A.D. 354-418), who appeared in Rome in the early part of the fifth century. Pelagius taught that children were not born sinners, in contradiction to Romans 5:12. Pelagius taught that children learned and chose to be sinners from the influences of those around them. Although children learn and choose to be sinners from the influences of those around them, this does not mean they were not born with a sin nature and are not therefore *sinners by nature*. Pelagius taught a person was not a sinner until he sinned.

As is the case in many of these theological debates (*logical debates*), the *pendulum only stops at the extremes*. The debate forced both parties into extreme and unscriptural logical presuppositions that lacked any solid Biblical exegesis. Therefore, both were wrong.

Pelagius' teaching went as far as to teach that it was possible to live a sinless life and that some people lived their whole lives without sinning. Obviously, this is false according to the Word of God. "If we say that we have no sin, we deceive ourselves, and the truth is not in us" (I John 1:8**). Pelagius' teaching was based upon the logic of human observation, not upon the exegesis of Scripture.** Although there are people that live very moral lives externally, many people forget that sin comes in three categories. All three of these categories of sin are found in the list of the "works of the flesh" in Galatians 5:19-21.

1. Sins of the flesh (actions of moral turpitude)
2. Sins of the heart (carnal emotional reactions and desires)
3. Sins of the mind (carnal thoughts, false beliefs, and vile imaginations)

"[19] Now the **works of the flesh are manifest**, which are *these*; Adultery, fornication, uncleanness, lasciviousness, [20] Idolatry, witchcraft, hatred, variance, emulations, wrath, strife, seditions, heresies, [21] Envyings, murders, drunkenness, revellings, and **such like** {*not exhaustive, but representative*}: of the which I tell you before, as I have also told *you* in time past, that **they which do** {*prásso, habitually practice or perform habitually*} such things shall not inherit the kingdom of God" (Galatians 5:19-21).

Pelagius was heretically wrong in saying that babies were not born sinners and that people could choose to live sinless lives. Pelagius was right in saying people learn to be sinners from their corporate ethic and are given social peer permission for sinful choices. Pelagius was right in teaching people could choose to make moral choices and had a free will to do so. However, Pelagius failed to understand the difference between making moral choices and being able to live the kind of righteousness that is God-like, which is perfect holiness absent of *thought sins* or *emotion sins*. A person might make a moral an external choice of restraint when his thought is murder, and his emotion is hatred. Thereby, that person chooses not to commit an act of sin before the eyes of the world, while committing the thought sin and emotional sin in the eyes of God.

Total depravity and spiritual death are not defined by inability. Spiritually dead people choose to sin. Spiritually dead people can also choose to live as morally as their "flesh" might be allow. However, **moral choices are choices.** The heart of preaching is intent on *convincing* (John 16:7-11) both spiritually dead men and regenerated men *to make right choices* (righteousness). Although all of humanity is lost in sin and is totally corrupt, spiritually blind (I Corinthians 2:9 and 14), and incapable of God-kind righteousness, God has not left sinners alone in the darkness (Romans 1:19-20).

"⁵ And the light shineth in darkness; and the darkness comprehended it not. ⁶ There was a man sent from God, whose name *was* John {*John the Baptist*}. ⁷ The same came for a witness, to bear witness of the Light, **that <u>all</u> men through him might** {*subjunctive mood means it is possible for all to*} **believe.** ⁸ He {*John the Baptist*} was not that Light, but *was sent* to bear witness of that Light. ⁹ *That* was the true Light, **which lighteth** {*enables to* *see or illuminates}* <u>**every man**</u> **that cometh into the world**" (John 1:5-9).

God's expectation of perfect righteousness and man's failure and inability to achieve that perfect righteousness has been a spiritual constant since the fall of Adam and his corruption with a sin nature. **This spiritual constant is what Biblically defines humanity's total depravity.** Humans, whether "born again" or not, are totally depraved in the sense no one can live the kind of perfect righteousness that God is apart from God's enabling through the ministry of His Spirit.

However, this does NOT nullify the fact that God has given all humans an inward conscience testifying to God's existence AND by which the external operations of God's Spirit uses God's Word internally to *prick the heart* bringing *guilt for sin* and *conviction* of inherent unrighteousness. **The very nature of the existence of *guilt* and *conviction* for sin when confronted with the Word of God are testimonies against total depravity being defined as total inability.** *Guilt* and *conviction* are the instruments of the Spirit of God to move sinners to make moral choices, to understand they are lost in their sins, and to seek God's solution to their hopeless dilemma in God's appointed Savior (Genesis 3:15). **It is the grace of God that brings all sinners to the threshold of choice.**

Biblically, *total depravity* is defined as the absolute inability to live in perfect righteousness that is as holy as God is holy and as God commands, "Be ye holy; for I am holy" (I Peter 1:16). No descendent of Adam can live a perfectly righteous life because he/she is born in sin with a sin nature that inwardly corrupts their hearts with lust sins and corrupts their minds with thought sins. No one who possesses a sin nature is exempt from total depravity, and all have a sin nature. This is the emphasis of both Romans 3:23 and Romans 5:12. Everyone is born condemned into a condemned world and everyone needs a Savior. Secondly, every "born again" sinner needs the Enabler to help him/her to live righteously. **Righteousness cannot come forth from a corrupted fountain.**

About a thousand years after Augustine and Pelagius, Martin Luther (A.D. 1483-1546) wrote a book on total depravity entitled *Bondage of the Will* in A.D. 1525. **Luther emphatically denied that any lost person had a free will.** Luther's book was written to vilify Desiderius Erasmus (A.D. 1466-1536) who had written a diatribe against what Luther had been teaching publicly. Desiderius Erasmus' book was entitled *Of Free Will: Discourses or Comparisons* (written A.D. 1524). These books are still available in their English translations and are often available free in PDF online.

The theology of Luther's *Bondage of the Will* would become the theological primer for most Reformed churches and continues so even unto today, although most Reformed people have not read it. Luther's *Bondage of the Will* is radical to the point that humans are so extremely depraved they cannot even exercise faith to be "born again." Luther went as far as to say a lost person cannot understand an iota of Scripture until he was *regenerated*.

The Reformed position taught that because of the *Bondage of the Will*, regeneration MUST precede a choice to believe because in regeneration God gifts the person elected/chosen to be regenerated the ability to believe and repent. **The paradox of this position was that most Reformed people believed in *baptismal regeneration*.** This means they believed that the baptism with the Spirit and the indwelling of the Spirit happens when a person is water *baptized* and usually referred to *infant baptism*, which required neither a choice of faith by the infant nor obviously any cognizance of sin or any form of repentance, but rather was considered viable based on the faith of the parents petitioning the Church for the sacrament.

This defines the Reformed teaching of *sovereign grace* or *irresistible grace.* Almost every form of professing Christianity believes salvation is by grace alone through faith. However, the terms *sovereign grace* or *irresistible grace* define saving grace in ways that have no Biblical foundation (*exegesis*) and read these presuppositions into Scripture (*eisegesis*). **The single defining term for God's choosing/electing certain people unconditionally to be regenerated and then in that regeneration gifting them the ability to choose to believe and repent, is the term** ***Monergism.*** One cannot discuss saving grace without delineation of the terms *sovereign grace, irresistible grace, and/or Monergism.*

Monergism is predominantly connected to Lutheranism, Calvinism, Presbyterianism, parts of the Church of England (Anglicanism), Dutch Reformed, Puritans, and even Reformed Baptists. Monergism has crept into many local churches through pastoral transitions and through congregational ignorance of terminology and of basic rules of hermeneutics.

Calvinism and its ***Monergism*** **is a theology of** ***pseudo-intellectualism*** **and is spread through the arrogant pride of that** ***pseudo-intellectualism.*** No where is that arrogant pride more evident than in Luther's condescending spite towards Erasmus in the books they wrote responding to the teachings of one to another.

Pretemporal (*before time began*) Reprobation
of the Non-elect

The Calvinist believes and teaches that the *non-elect* (those not chosen by God to be saved) are *reprobates* before they were ever even born, and God has predestined them to that fate before time was created. These reprobates are hopelessly lost because God will not regenerate them and give them the ability to believe and repent. Is this what the Word of God teaches?

Scriptural evidence reveals that reprobation, i.e., when God gives people over to a *reprobate mind*, is the ultimate end of a continuum of personal choices of digressively rejecting God's revelation. **No one is pretemporally reprobate!**

"[19] Because **that which may be known of God** {*God consciousness*} **is manifest in them** {*all lost people*}; for **God hath shewed** {*rendered His existence apparent*} *it* unto them. [20] For **the invisible things** {*the spiritual realm of things*} of him **from the creation** of the world **are clearly seen**, being understood by the things that are made, *even* his eternal power and Godhead; so that they are without excuse: [21] Because that, when they knew God, they glorified *him* not as God, neither were thankful; but became **vain in their imaginations**, and their foolish heart was darkened. [22] Professing themselves to be wise, they became fools, [23] **And changed the glory of the uncorruptible God** {*who and was God really is*} into an image made like to corruptible man, and to birds, and fourfooted beasts, and creeping things. [24] **Wherefore God also <u>gave them up</u> to uncleanness** through the lusts of their own hearts, to dishonour their own bodies between themselves: [25] Who **changed** {*exchanged*} **the truth of God into a lie** {*a falsehood*}, and worshipped and **served the creature** {*the creation of their falsehood*} more than the Creator, who is blessed for ever. Amen. [26] **For this cause God <u>gave them up</u> unto vile affections**: for even their women did change the natural use into that which is against nature: [27] And likewise also the men, leaving the natural use of the woman, burned in their lust one toward another; men with men working that which is unseemly, and receiving in themselves that recompence of their error which was meet. [28] And even as **they did not like to retain God in *their* knowledge, <u>God gave them over</u> to a reprobate** {*worthless deserving to be cast away*} **mind** {*one devoid of conscience and therefore completely dysfunctional, sociopathic*}, to do those things which are not convenient; [29] **Being filled** {*play-ro'-o*} **with all** unrighteousness, fornication, wickedness, covetousness, maliciousness; full of envy, murder, debate, deceit, malignity; whisperers, [30] Backbiters, haters of God, despiteful, proud, boasters, inventors of evil things, disobedient to parents, [31] **Without understanding**, covenantbreakers, without natural affection, implacable {*truceless*}, unmerciful: [32] Who knowing the judgment of God, that they which commit such things are worthy of death, not only do the same, but have pleasure in them that do them" (Romans 1:19-32).

Reprobation is different from condemnation. All reprobates are condemned, but not all condemned people are reprobates. Under Calvinism's teaching, only a few of the condemned are chosen to be regenerated.

"[1] This know also, that in the last days perilous times shall come. [2] For men shall **be lovers of their own selves** {*their own god*}, covetous, boasters, proud, blasphemers, disobedient to parents, unthankful, unholy, [3] Without natural affection, trucebreakers, false accusers, incontinent, fierce, despisers of those that are good, [4] Traitors, heady, highminded, lovers of pleasures more than lovers of God; [5] Having a form of godliness, but denying the power thereof: from such turn away. [6] For of this sort are they which creep into houses, and lead captive silly women laden with sins, led away with divers lusts, [7] Ever learning, and never able to come to the knowledge of the truth. [8] Now as Jannes and Jambres withstood Moses, so do these also resist the truth: **men of corrupt minds, reprobate concerning the faith**" (II Timothy 3:1-8).

"They profess that they know God; but in works they deny *him*, being abominable, and disobedient, and **unto every good work reprobate**" (Titus 1:16).

Scripturally, a reprobate is a person without a working conscience and who is no longer sensitive to the convicting of the Holy Spirit. No one is born reprobate, and no one is pretemporally reprobate. However, within Calvinism and their *bondage of the will* of those God has **not** elected/chosen unto salvation, God will not regenerate them and will not give them the ability to respond in faith and repent. For the Calvinist, the order of salvation is God choosing/electing certain people unconditionally and without merit, regenerating those elected at some unspecified time without their knowledge or consent, giving them the ability to believe and repent, and preserving them through practical sanctification until they are finally glorified. **Calvinists teach that all of this is predestined for those God has chosen/elected. Ichabod!**

God's Sovereignty is not the same as *Sovereign Grace* teaching

Calvinism's false doctrine of *total depravity* logically demands their solution in *unconditional election* and *sovereign grace*. They believe that since humanity is "dead in trespasses and sins" (Ephesians 2:1) that dead men cannot believe or repent. They believe that dead men must be given life, faith, and repentance through regeneration *before* they can understand, repent, and believe (*Monergism*). However, these gifts will be given only to those God has elected to be regenerated. **This defines Calvinism's *sovereign grace* doctrine. All this is unbiblical.**

When talking about salvation being available to anyone willing to make a faith decision to be "born again," the Calvinist will almost get angry over this teaching labeling anyone that would posit such an absurdity as ignorant at best or an idiot at worse. Such people are immediately labeled *Arminians* or *Pelagians*. For Calvinists, salvation is solely God's choice and *sovereign grace* means God must regenerate before a person can believe. The elect have no part whatsoever in their regeneration. For them, regeneration is not the outcome of a faith decision, regeneration enables a person to repent and believe so they can make a faith decision.

Trying to understand, let alone describe, God's sovereignty is pretty much an operation in futility. Can the finite comprehend the infinite? However, we can be confident that sovereign grace is *not* as defined by Calvinists as detailed in the above paragraphs. Sovereignty defines God's Lordship/Dominion over His creation and the beings within that creation. Sovereignty is primarily a judicial term connected to God's judgments.

Even when the Infinite One seeks to aid us with revelation of Himself in considerable detail, we must admit that no matter how logical and meticulous we try to be in interpreting all the data provided, we are going to miserably fail in being able to systematize it all into a congruous and harmonious understanding of Who God is and in understanding how He operates. This has been the failure of all logical systems of theology such as Augustinianism, Calvinism, and Arminianism as well as all the self-propagating constituents of these systems of logic. The problem begins the moment we take logic or rationalism one-step beyond the revelation of the inspired Scriptures.

Like a pendulum, logical systems of theology only stop at the extremes. The logical systems of theology (using *Aristotelian Syllogism*) always lead adherents into extremes. Logical systems of theology such as Augustinianism and Calvinism lead adherents to the extreme of *closed theism* (*Determinism* or *Fatalism*). Logical systems of theology such as Arminianism lead adherents to the extreme of *open theism* (*Neo-theism, Chaos* or, *Deism*). Most theologians following either of these systems of logic attempt to argue themselves away from the extremes. Some merely accept the extremes and propagate them as the only acceptable truth labeling any other position as heretical.

Dispensationalist and Covenant Theologians have all had their own problems and variations of discussion around the issue of God's sovereignty. These discussions have been wide and diverse in their approaches to this issue. Within Dispensationalism, the theological discussion of God's sovereignty (*Lordship/dominion/Judgeship*) centers on the discussion of the Kingdom of God and the Kingdom of Heaven and how God's sovereignty is practically manifested in and through these two Kingdoms and how God's sovereignty differs and/or interrelates. **The sovereignty of God means He governs/rules/judges in righteousness.**

"[26] Then came **the word of the LORD** {*Jehovah; the eternal self-existing Sovereign of all that is or shall be*} unto Jeremiah, saying, [27] **Behold, I *am* the LORD, the God of all flesh: is there any thing too hard for me?** [28] Therefore thus saith the LORD; Behold, I will give this city into the hand of the Chaldeans, and into the hand of Nebuchadrezzar king of Babylon, and he shall take it: [29] And the Chaldeans, that fight against this city, shall come and set fire on this city, and burn it with the houses, upon whose roofs they have offered incense unto Baal, and poured out drink offerings unto other gods, to provoke me to anger. [30] For the children of Israel and the children of Judah have only done evil before me from their youth: for **the children of Israel have only provoked me to anger with the work of their hands, saith the LORD**" (Jerimiah 32:26-30).

The discussion on God's sovereignty varies in the understanding of these two Kingdoms between *Traditional Dispensationalists, Revised Dispensationalists,* and *Progressive Dispensationalists, and Covenant Theologians.* Many individuals, who claim to be Dispensationalists and who are part of all three of these variations of Dispensationalism, may also consider themselves in varying degrees of Reformed Theology in their soteriology. Most *New Light Presbyterians* moved from Covenant Theology to dispensational theology also accepting "God-centered" revivalism according to the *Great Awakening* (the likes of Johnathan Edwards and George Whitfield) while retaining their *Reformed Sovereign Grace* position regarding *Monergism.*

Many of the *New Light Baptist* congregations were formed by Congregationalists, although still Calvinists, were convinced that infant baptism was unscriptural. They still rejected the *decisional revivalism* of the *Second Awakening* through men like Charles Finney, who was definitely Pelagian (believed no one was a sinner until he/she sinned). Finney invented the *Anxious Bench* or the *Mourners Bench* where people would come to the front of the assembly and then be led by a counselor to make a rational decision to repent and believe to be "born again." Charles Finney was rejected by both *New Light* and *Old Light* Presbyterians for his views and practices.

Many of these so-called *salvation decisions* lacked the foundation of careful explanation of what the death, burial, and resurrection of Christ accomplished for

sinners and therefore the decisions to receive Christ lacked the foundation of understanding, thereby creating a huge percentage of professing Christians committed to *piety* **without having been genuinely "born again."** This would later develop into the *easy prayerism* of many Baptist congregations (*Roman's Road* and *pray this prayer*) and other variations of *soteriological reductionism* in most of Evangelicalism. In this development of *soteriological reductionism,* a Biblical response to the Gospel of Jesus Christ was almost completely lost (*repent, believe, confess, call*, and *receive*, Romans 10:1-13 and John 1:11-12).

The Corporate/Vocational View of Election
Chapter Four
God's Sovereignty

Traditional or classic dispensationalists saw the Kingdom of God and the Kingdom of Heaven as *distinct* from one another. This position would have included such men as John N. Darby, Clarence Larkin, C.I. Scofield, Lewis S. Chafer, and Charles C. Ryrie (in the 1950s).[17] This *classic dispensational* position would have aligned with the notes in the original 1917 edition of the Scofield Reference Bible.

The revised dispensationalists of the 1950's through the 1970's revised the traditional position on the two Kingdoms in two ways.[18] The editors of the *New Scofield Reference Bible* took the position that the Kingdom of God and the Kingdom of Heaven were *interchangeable, but distinct.* Others taking this revised position were Alva J. McClain, J. Dwight Pentecost, and John F. Walvoord. Others of this period saw the two Kingdoms as *synonymous with no distinction.* This would have included Eric Sauer, Clarence E. Mason, Charles C. Ryrie (who changed his position in the 1970's), and Stanley D. Toussaint.[19]

Classic or traditional dispensationalists see a clear distinction between the Kingdom of God and the Kingdom of Heaven. The problem that creates the other two positions is the failure to see *levels* of sovereignty as decreed by God. When God "created the heaven and the earth" (Genesis 1:1), He created a physical existence that was

---

[17] Herbert W. Bateman IV, General Editor, *Three Central Issues in Contemporary Dispensationalism*, Kregal Publications, Grand Rapids, Michigan, page 30.

[18] Ibid.

[19] Ibid.

considerably different than the existence in which He was/is. **God is sovereign over both existences.** God is certainly sovereign over His own eternal existence and all that dwell with Him in that eternal spiritual existence. The *Kingdom of Heaven(s)* is a created existence of time, space, and matter. **God retains sovereignty over the Kingdom of the Heavens as well and judges in righteousness.**

"[1] In **the third month**, when the children of Israel were gone forth out of the land of Egypt, the same day came they *into* the wilderness of Sinai. [2] For they were departed from Rephidim, and were come *to* the desert of Sinai, and had pitched in the wilderness; and there Israel camped before the mount. [3] And **Moses went up unto God**, and the LORD called unto him out of the mountain, saying, **Thus shalt thou say to the house of Jacob, and tell the children of Israel**; [4] Ye have seen what I did unto the Egyptians, and *how* I bare you on eagles' wings, and brought you unto myself. [5] Now therefore, **if** ye will obey my voice indeed, and keep my covenant, **then** ye shall be a peculiar treasure unto me above all people: **for all the earth *is* mine:** [6] And **ye shall be unto me a kingdom of priests, and an holy nation**. These *are* the words which thou shalt speak unto the children of Israel" (Exodus 19:1-6).

God originally gave sovereignty ("dominion") of the *Kingdom of Heaven(s)* to Adam who relinquished that sovereignty to Satan when Adam chose to disobey God and yielded to sin. Therefore, the Kingdom of God and the Kingdom of Heaven are distinct. However, the Kingdom of Heaven (time,. space, and matter) continues to be under the sovereignty of God in that God has retained the authority of both judgment and condemnation within this lesser Kingdom of Heaven. We know this because, although God gave dominion of the original creation (the Kingdom of Heaven) to Adam, God retained *dominion* or *sovereignty* over Adam when God retained *sovereignty* over "the tree of the knowledge of good and evil" (Genesis 2:17) and cursed the first creation.

Therefore, when Adam relinquished the dominion of the Kingdom of Heaven to Satan and Satan became "the prince of the power of the air" (Ephesians 2:2), God retained sovereignty over Satan and could curse him and condemn the original creation to destruction (Genesis 3:14-19). Dispensationalism then becomes the historical paradigms through which God will restore dominion of the Kingdom of Heaven through the incarnation of the Son of God and through His death, burial, resurrection, glorification, and return to earth as the *Last Adam* of the New Genesis "in Christ." The *Jamieson-Fausset-Brown Commentary* gives an excellent explanation of all this:

> **"the prince of the power of the air**--the unseen God who lies underneath guiding 'the course of this world' (2Co 4:4); ranging through the *air* around us: compare Mr 4:4, 'fowls of the air' (*Greek,* 'heaven') that is, (Eph 2:15), 'Satan' and his demons. Compare Eph 6:12; Joh 12:31. Christ's ascension seems to have cast Satan out of heaven (Re 12:5,9-10,12-13), where he had been heretofore the accuser of the brethren (Job 1:6-11). No longer able to accuse *in heaven* those justified by Christ, the ascended Saviour (Ro 8:33-34), he assails them on earth with all trials and temptations; and 'we live in an atmosphere poisonous and impregnated with deadly elements. But a mighty purification of the air will be effected by Christ's coming' [AUBERLEN], for Satan shall be bound (Re 12:12-13,15; 20:2-3). 'The power' is here used collectively for the 'powers of the air'; in apposition with which 'powers' stand the 'spirits,'

comprehended in the singular, 'the spirit,' taken also collectively: the aggregate of the 'seducing spirits' (1Ti 4:1) which 'work now (*still;* not merely, as in your case, 'in time *past*') in the sons of disobedience' (a Hebraism: men who are not merely by accident disobedient, but who are essentially *sons of disobedience* itself: compare Mt 3:7), and of which Satan is here declared to be 'the prince.' The *Greek* does not allow 'the spirit' to refer to *Satan,* 'the prince' himself, but to '*the powers of the air*' of which he is prince. The powers of the air are the embodiment of that evil 'spirit' which is the ruling principle of unbelievers, especially the heathen (Ac 26:18), as opposed to the spirit of the children of God (Lu 4:33). The potency of that 'spirit' is shown in the 'disobedience' of the former. Compare De 32:20, 'children in whom is no faith' (Isa 30:9; 57:4). They disobey the Gospel both in faith and practice (2Th 1:8; 2Co 2:12)."[20]

These two kingdoms (Kingdom of God and Kingdom of Heaven) will always be distinct in that God will ultimately destroy the original creation. Then the "born again" souls of Kingdom of Heaven over which Christ reigns sovereign will be *melded* into the Kingdom of God in "the regeneration" and the creation of a New Heaven/Earth.

Sovereignty equals God's pretemporal judgments in righteousness upon the cursed world and all who reject His gift of the regeneration through faith in Christ.

---

[20] *Commentary Critical and Explanatory on the Whole Bible,* Robert Jamieson, A.R. Fausset, and David Brown, 1871. Abridged, single-volume edition. SwordSearcher\Modules\JFB.ss5cmty, Module file time: 8/2/2021 11:33:18 PM UTC.

Within the varying circles of Covenant Theology (including both Calvinism and Arminianism), the *theological* (pronounced: in-tl-**ek**-choo-uhl) discussion in this arena of logic involving God's sovereignty usually centers on the meaning of words such as *decreed, determined, ordained, foreordained, appointed,* and, *predestined.* **The problems develop when the grammatical definitions of these words are taken beyond their contextual applications in Scripture.**

Logic is naturally *anthropomorphic* (reasoning within *Empiricism*). Secondly, logic tends to treat *infinite* things as *finite* things and *incomprehensible* things as *comprehensible.* Therefore, logic is fatally flawed as a methodology to establish a Systematic Theology. (This does not mean that theology is *illogical* or *alogical.*) Thirdly, logic often results in *eisegesis*; logical suppositions of meaning are taken beyond Biblical usage and these meanings are then interjected into the interpretation of Scripture. Such is the case when Calvinists take the verse, "for God so loved the world," and interject their presuppositions regarding election to make the verse say, "for God so loved *the elect*;" or when the Word of God's says "whosoever," they interpret that to mean "whosoever *of the elect*." **Any degree of this nonsense is suicide to Biblical exegesis ("rightly dividing the Word of truth").**

Calvinists tend to be monothetic regarding God's sovereignty or will. For the Calvinist, whatever God has decreed, willed, commanded, or ordained **must** happen. **What God decrees, God must *cause* to happen.** Calvinists cannot separate God's foreknowledge of future events from God's ordination/decrees in His prophetic revelation of His unfolding historical *Plan of the Ages.* In this Monothetic approach, God's sovereignty (Lordship) must translate into God's mastery (control).

"**Monothetic and Polythetic Definitions** - deriving from Greek for either one, alone (*mono-*) or many, much (*poly-*) that are 'capable of placing,' as in one-placement and many-placements. Monothetic definitions, which can be essentialist or functionalist, presume a limited set of necessary characteristics or purposes whereas polythetic (or what might also be termed multi-factoral) definitions identify a range of traits or functions, none of which is sufficient in order for the object to qualify as a member of a class."[21]

The fact is that the Scriptural pattern is usually just the opposite of this monothetic view of God's sovereignty/will. What God *really* is in His existence does not necessarily translate into what God *practically* is in the believer's life and in this world. What do I mean by that? **Simply, God's will is not always obeyed. God's authority/sovereignty/Lordship can be rejected. This is called rebellion.**

We can emphatically declare that Jesus is Lord (the Sovereign). He is ALWAYS Lord, whether a person acknowledges and submits to His Lordship or not. The practical issue of Christ's Lordship has to do with a believer yielding his will to the will of God (Romans 6:11-13). This does not MAKE Christ Lord. Neither does yielding bring the believer's life within or under the Lordship of Christ because all lives always exist under the Lordship of Christ. Yielding merely reaps the practical benefits of the Lordship of Christ upon the yielded believer's life.

"The term Lord in Acts 16:31 - or anywhere else it is used of Christ - does not mean Master over one's life.

---

[21] (http://www.as.ua.edu/rel/aboutreldefinitions.html)

Rather it is a descriptive title of who He is - the sovereign God"[22]

There is a significant difference in the meaning of the words *control* and *cause*. The pre-determination of something happening (to determine outcomes beforehand, foreknowledge; knowledge of what will *actually* happen in time before it *actually* happens in time) is not the same as *causing* something to happen. If I know all the facts about something, I can *determine* and *foreknow* the outcome without *causing* the outcome.

For instance, a drunkard gets into a car with a .2 blood/alcohol level. He will drive that car more than 120 miles an hour on a curved road. The road is icy in spots. A deer will jump out of the woods at mile marker 121 just before a curve in the road near a ravine to the right side of the road on which the man is driving. The drunkard will swerve right to miss the deer. The drunkard will drive into that ravine and the steering wheel will crush his heart causing massive heart failure. From knowing all these facts, I can *predetermine* the outcome. The more perfect my knowledge, the more perfect is my *predetermination*. The question then must be raised; just because I foreknew all the details, was I in any way the cause of his death?

This leads us to a dictionary and grammatical definition of *sovereignty*. In most part, the definition of *sovereignty* has more to do with *authority* or *Lordship* than it has to do with *cause* or *control*. God's *sovereignty* has more to do with Him *regulating* His creation than controlling/causing every decision.

---

[22] Robert Lightner: *Sin, the Savior, and Salvation: The Theology of Everlasting Life.* Kregel Publications, 1991, Grand Rapids, Mich., page 206.

This does not mean God is not exerting His influence on every decision or, that in certain cases, He does not override certain decisions by divine interference. God is certainly involved in both the *macromanagement* and *micromanagement* of the affairs of this world. Undoubtedly, God is sovereign. However, discovering how God's sovereignty extends into God's creation is how we must define God's sovereignty.

sov·er·eign·ty (*n. pl.* **sov·er·eign·ties**)
1. Supremacy of authority or rule as exercised by a sovereign or sovereign state.
2. Royal rank, authority, or power.
3. Complete independence and self-government.
4. A territory existing as an independent state.[23]

Sov·er·eign·ty: Variant: *also* **sov·ran·ty** /'sä-vr&n-tE, 's&-, -v&-r&n-/
Function: *noun;* Inflected Form: *plural* **–ties**
1 a : supreme power esp. over a body politic **b :** freedom from external control
2 : one that is sovereign; *especially* : an autonomous state[24]

Sovereignty of God, his absolute right to do all things according to His own good pleasure (Dan. 4:25, 35; Rom. 9:15-23; 1 Tim. 6:15; Rev. 4:11).[25]

---

[23] *Source: The American Heritage® Dictionary of the English Language, Fourth Edition Copyright © 2000 by Houghton Mifflin Company. Published by Houghton Mifflin Company.*
[24] Source: *Merriam-Webster's Dictionary of Law,* © 1996 Merriam-Webster, Inc.
[25] Source: *Easton's 1897 Bible Dictionary*

"Sovereignty in government is that public authority
which directs or orders what is to be done by each
member associated in relation to the end of the
association. It is the supreme power by which any
citizen is governed and is the person or body of persons
in the state to whom there is politically no superior. The
necessary existence of the state and that right and power
which necessarily follow is 'sovereignty.' By
'sovereignty' in its largest sense is meant supreme,
absolute, uncontrollable power, the absolute right to
govern. The word which by itself comes nearest to
being the definition of 'sovereignty' is will or volition
as applied to political affairs."[26]

Sovereignty is primarily a term of governance. In
secular use, it relates primarily to issues of law, government,
and jurisprudence. Theologically, the word carries similar
meaning. Understanding this defines the issue of God's
absolute will as it relates to man's will (individual soul
liberty). **Defining these issues can only be accomplished
through understanding the application of these terms
within the context of that use in Scripture. The context is
exemplary and resultantly definitive.** We must be cautious
not to read more into the definition of sovereignty than the
examples of historical application and revelatory statements
allow. This moves us first to the definition of theism.

"Theism denotes a supernatural, infinite, personal Being
who created the material universe and who transcends
it. The theist God can and does intervene in the world
in a supernatural way from time to time."[27]

---

[26] Source: *Black's Law Dictionary; Sixth Edition.*
[27] Norman L. Geisler, H. Wayne House with Max Herrera, *The Battle for
God*, Kregel Publications, Grand Rapids, Mich., 2001, page 8.

Theism is the cognizance of who God is, what He has done, what He is doing, and involves the believer in discerning God through the revelation of His past interventions within His creation and in interaction with His creatures. However, theism becomes finite and philosophical in its definitions of who God is when we consider it involves the finite human cognizance of an infinite God.

> "The ETYMOLOGY of the word *theism* would give it a wide application, but in common usage it has come to mean a belief in God, and incorporates a system of beliefs which constitutes a philosophy, restricted, indeed, somewhat to those findings and conclusions which human reason suggests. . . In the Bible, man is ever reminded of the fact of his own limitations and of the knowledge-surpassing perfections of God. Antitheistic agnosticism has taken refuge in the denial of divine cognizability; but there is a true knowledge of God – true as far as it is able to go – which does not fully comprehend its subject. Such incompleteness, indeed, may be predicated of very much if not all of human cognizance. In his defense of antitheistic agnosticism, Hamilton declared: 'The last and highest consecration of all true religion must be an altar . . . to the unknown or unknowable God.' "[28]

This is not to say that theism cannot be definitive/dogmatic to a great degree. Although God is incomprehensible, He is knowable to the degree He has revealed Himself through Scripture and His historical

---

[28] Lewis Sperry Chafer, *Systematic Theology, Vol. I*, Zondervan Publishing House, Grand Rapids, Mich., page 137, 138.

interactions with humanity. Exegesis is about the careful evaluation and discernment of God's revelation regarding His attributes and character. Therefore, logic and human reason must take extreme care in not going beyond God's revelation of Himself to extrapolate a *God* that really does not exist, thereby creating a philosophical *idol*.

To begin a study of God's sovereignty, we must begin with the *beginning* of His revelation, i.e., Genesis. "In the beginning God" issued various sovereign decrees. **He said, "let there be" and there was.** God's decrees are relevant to the way God governs His creation. God has creative decrees where He causes what He decrees and physical decrees (the Laws of Physics) where He creates a system of laws by which His creation subsists or by which it is governed. The sovereign degrees of God's creation encompass all the Laws of Physics that govern God's creation. The sovereignty of God includes both the sovereignty of God's revealed and predestined judgments as well as God's revealed sovereign grace to humanity.

"[9] And God said, Let the waters under the heaven be gathered together unto one place, and let the dry *land* appear: and it was so. [10] And God called the dry *land* Earth; and the gathering together of the waters called he Seas: and God saw that *it was* good. [11] And God said, Let the earth bring forth grass, the herb yielding seed, *and* the fruit tree yielding fruit after his kind, whose seed *is* in itself, upon the earth: and it was so. [12] And the earth brought forth grass, *and* herb yielding seed after his kind, and the tree yielding fruit, whose seed *was* in itself, after his kind: and God saw that *it was* good" (Genesis 1:9-12).

"[22] Destruction and death say, We have heard the fame thereof with our ears. [23] God understandeth the way thereof, and he knoweth the place thereof. [24] For he looketh to the ends of the earth, *and* seeth under the whole heaven; [25] To make the weight for the winds; and he weigheth the waters by measure. [26] When **he made a decree for the rain**, and a way for the lightning of the thunder: [27] Then did he see it, and declare it; he prepared it, yea, and searched it out" (Job 28:22-27).

"[4] Where wast thou when I laid the foundations of the earth? declare, if thou hast understanding. [5] Who hath laid the measures thereof, if thou knowest? or who hath stretched the line upon it? [6] Whereupon are the foundations thereof fastened? or who laid the corner stone thereof; [7] When the morning stars sang together, and all the sons of God shouted for joy? [8] Or *who* shut up the sea with doors, when it brake forth, *as if* it had issued out of the womb? [9] When I made the cloud the garment thereof, and thick darkness a swaddlingband for it, [10] And brake up for it my decreed *place*, and set bars and doors, [11] And said, Hitherto shalt thou come, but no further: and here shall thy proud waves be stayed? [12] Hast thou commanded the morning since thy days; *and* caused the dayspring to know his place; [13] That it might take hold of the ends of the earth, that the wicked might be shaken out of it? [14] It is turned as clay *to* the seal; and they stand as a garment. [15] And from the wicked their light is withholden, and the high arm shall be broken. [16] Hast thou entered into the springs of the sea? or hast thou walked in the search of the depth? [17] Have the gates of death been opened unto thee? or hast thou seen the doors of the shadow of death? [18] Hast thou perceived the breadth of the earth? declare if thou knowest it all. [19] Where *is* the way *where* light dwelleth? and *as for* darkness, where *is* the place thereof, [20] That thou shouldest take it to the bound thereof, and that thou shouldest know the paths *to* the house thereof? [21] Knowest thou *it*, because thou wast then born? or *because* the number of thy days *is* great? [22] Hast thou entered into the treasures of the snow? or hast thou seen the treasures of the hail, [23] Which I have reserved against the time of trouble, against the day of battle and war? [24] By what way is the light parted, *which* scattereth the east wind upon the earth? [25] Who hath divided a watercourse for the overflowing of waters, or a way for the lightning of thunder; [26] To cause it to rain on the earth, *where* no man *is; on* the wilderness, wherein *there is* no man; [27] To satisfy the desolate and waste *ground*; and to cause the bud of the tender herb to spring forth? [28] Hath the rain a father? or who hath begotten the drops of dew? [29] Out of whose womb came the ice? and the hoary frost of heaven, who hath gendered it? [30] The waters are hid as *with* a stone, and the face of the deep is frozen. [31] Canst thou bind the sweet influences of Pleiades, or loose the bands of Orion? [32] Canst thou bring forth Mazzaroth in his season? or canst thou guide Arcturus with his sons? [33] Knowest thou the ordinances of heaven? canst thou set the dominion thereof in the earth? [34] Canst thou lift up thy voice to the clouds, that abundance of waters may cover thee? [35] Canst thou send lightnings, that they may go, and say unto thee, Here we *are*? [36] Who hath put wisdom in the inward parts? or who hath given understanding to the heart? [37] Who can number the clouds in wisdom? or who can stay the bottles of heaven, [38] When the dust groweth into hardness, and the clods cleave fast together? [39] Wilt thou hunt the prey for the lion? or fill the appetite of the young lions, [40] When they couch in *their* dens, *and* abide in the covert to lie in wait? [41] Who provideth for the raven his food? when his young ones cry unto God, they wander for lack of meat" (Job 38:4-41).

"²² The LORD possessed me {*wisdom*} in the beginning of his way, before his works of old. ²³ I was set up from everlasting, from the beginning, or ever the earth was. ²⁴ When *there were* no depths, I was brought forth; when *there were* no fountains abounding with water. ²⁵ Before the mountains were settled, before the hills was I brought forth: ²⁶ While as yet he had not made the earth, nor the fields, nor the highest part of the dust of the world. ²⁷ When he prepared the heavens, I *was* there: when he set a compass upon the face of the depth: ²⁸ When he established the clouds above: when he strengthened the fountains of the deep: ²⁹ **When he gave to the sea his decree**, that the waters should not pass his commandment: when he appointed the foundations of the earth: ³⁰ **Then I was by him, *as* one brought up with him**: and I was daily *his* delight, rejoicing always before him; ³¹ Rejoicing in the habitable part of his earth; and my delights *were* with the sons of men" (Proverbs 8:22-31).

"²¹ Hear now this, O foolish people, and without understanding; which have eyes, and see not; which have ears, and hear not: ²² Fear ye not me? saith the LORD: will ye not tremble at my presence, which have **placed the sand *for* the bound of the sea by a perpetual decree**, that it cannot pass it: and though the waves thereof toss themselves, yet can they not prevail; though they roar, yet can they not pass over it" (Jeremiah 5:21-22)?

There are also judicial decrees from God. This is the primary meaning of the word *decree* in Scripture. All of God's commandments would come under this category of God's *decrees*. It is important to note that judicial decrees carry with them judicial consequences, should they be disobeyed. Soul liberty is relevant only to God's judicial decrees. The first of these judicial decrees is found in Genesis 2:15-17.

"[15] And the LORD God took the man, and put him into the garden of Eden to dress it and to keep it. [16] And the LORD God commanded the man, saying, Of every tree of the garden thou mayest freely eat: [17] But of the tree of the knowledge of good and evil, thou shalt not eat of it: for in the day that thou eatest thereof thou shalt surely die" (Genesis 2:15-17).

An important issue here is that both the transcendence of God's sovereignty and His immanency are embodied in the decree given by God to Adam in Genesis 2:16-17. Although God gave Adam dominion over all God's creation, God retained His dominion over Adam's soul and the souls of all mankind in Adam.

"Behold, all souls are mine; as the soul of the father, so also the soul of the son is mine: the soul that sinneth, it shall die" (Ezekiel 18:4).

When God created Adam, He created him as a free moral agent. God created man with moral consciousness and with the knowledge of right and wrong and a conscience intended to direct man in making moral choices. The human conscience works *synergistically* with God's *known* judicial degrees and the *influence* of the Holy Spirit operating in the world. When the conscience comes to the place of a moral decision/choice, God's judicial decrees must be considered along with their consequences and a moral or immoral choice is made in the exercise of the *will* given by God to all mankind. When a man makes a decision of the will contrary to God's decree, the judicial consequences of that decision are enforced by God. The enforcement can come in the form of chastisement in this life, loss of rewards for a believer in eternity or, God's eternal judgment in the "second death" for the lost.

These three categories of decrees involve hundreds of individual decrees from God. Beyond these individual decrees we find an all-encompassing decree of God in the progressive unfolding of "the regeneration." We call this unfolding plan of God, *dispensationalism*. This "regeneration" is the eternal purpose in God's decrees *to His own glory*. All that God does within the time/space/matter of the original creation is to bring souls lost in the condemnation of the Adamic Fall into "the regeneration." Then, God seeks to bring believers into the full revelation of all that God is in His majestic attributes and character. Without this ministry of God to sinners, they would remain "blinded" by satanic deception and corruption of truth.

We might say that "the regeneration" is God's ultimate purpose in His eternal decree *to His own glory*. Each dispensation is an individual decree within God's eternal decree for the same purposes ("the regeneration" and bringing God glory). God's individual decrees are always in perfect alignment with His eternal decree down through the ages. Understanding how these decrees are fulfilled in the eternal plan of God and how God's purposes are realized within the human predicament of a fallen creation involves numerous factors. First, this involves God and all His attributes within the human predicament. This involves God's omnipotence, His omnipresence, and His omniscience. It involves the holiness that God is. It involves the love that God is. It involves the truth/wisdom that God is. It involves God's grace, longsuffering, gentleness, goodness, mercy, wrath, justice, and immutability.

Beside all of this, God has chosen/elected to use human agents *synergistically* in the realization of His

eternal plan. Historically, down through the ages, God has chosen/elected the nation of Israel, the Church, and individuals within these two elect groups to accomplish His decrees. He then anoints or fills (depending in which dispensation the individual lives) those individuals with His Holy Spirit to supernaturally enable them to fulfill the purposes to which they were/are called. The message of the Gospel and the promise of a Savior is a *hand-me-down truth* to which every new generation is both responsible and accountable to distribute and propagate, beginning with the message of Genesis 3:15 to the intricate details of the Gospel in the epistle to the Romans. Believers down through the ages are culpable for the dissemination of the message of God's redemption in the Promised One. This is one of God's decrees within His eternal decree.

"[18] And Jesus came and spake unto them, saying, All power is given unto me in heaven and in earth. [19] Go ye therefore, and teach all nations, baptizing them in the name of the Father, and of the Son, and of the Holy Ghost: [20] Teaching them to observe all things whatsoever I have commanded you: and, lo, I am with you alway, *even* unto the end of the world. Amen" (Matthew 28:18-20).

When considering God's sovereignty, it is important to differentiate between God's foreknowledge and God's foreordination. Some questions must be asked and answered. Does God foreknow the outcome of His eternal plan *because* He has foreordained/caused (predestined) every detail of history resulting in a predetermined outcome (Monothetism, Determinism, Monergism, or Fatalism)? Does God foreknow the outcome of His eternal plan merely *because* He is omniscient and knows all things actual and all things possible (Neo-theism)? Is God dependent upon human agents to accomplish His eternal plan and outcomes (Humanism)? Or is God actively involved in every minute detail of His creation through the omni-influence of His Spirit, through progressive revelation, through the ordination of kings, prophets, priests, apostles, evangelists, and pastors/teachers, through the judgment of nations and, through dispensational transitions (Synergistic Theism)? It seems apparent to me that this latter scenario is what we consistently see through the progressive revelation of God's Word.

We can answer these questions by quoting a number of proof texts taken out of context (Calvinism is primarily a *proof text theology*) or we can answer these questions with the overwhelming inductive evidence of historical examples provided to us by God through His progressive revelation of His operations within the human predicament (*Sola Scriptura*).

Would the earth ever have been populated if Adam and Eve had not obeyed God's decree to "be fruitful, multiply, and replenish the earth" (Genesis 1:28)? Did God cause them or force them to produce children, or did they *choose* to obey His decree? Where would mankind be today if Noah had not obeyed God's decree to build a giant boat for a flood that would come a hundred years later? Did God *cause* Noah or force Noah to build the Ark or did Noah choose to obey God's decree? Where would mankind be if God had not interfered in the judgment of the decadence of humanity through a universal flood? Did God *cause* or *force* the unbelieving world to reject His offer to go into the Ark or did they *choose* to disobey and reject His offer? We could go on and on.

The idea here is that God worked miraculously and intricately through hundreds/thousands/millions of human agents and their innumerable failures to accomplish His ultimate goals: to bring about "the regeneration" and bring glory to His Name. I believe this takes God's sovereignty to the infinite degree it deserves and the degree in which it exists. That God could instrument and orchestrate His ultimate purposes through all this only magnifies His attributes and infinitely glorifies Him throughout history.

"⁵ To whom will ye liken me, and make *me* equal, and compare me, that we may be like? ⁶ They lavish gold out of the bag, and weigh silver in the balance, *and* hire a goldsmith; and he maketh it a god: they fall down, yea, they worship. ⁷ They bear him upon the shoulder, they carry him, and set him in his place, and he standeth; from his place shall he not remove: yea, *one* shall cry unto him, yet can he not answer, nor save him out of his trouble. ⁸ Remember this, and shew yourselves men: bring *it* again to mind, O ye transgressors. ⁹ Remember the former things of old: for I *am* God, and *there is* none else; *I am* God, and *there is* none like me, ¹⁰ Declaring the end from the beginning, and from ancient times *the things* that are not *yet* done, saying, My counsel shall stand, and I will do all my pleasure: ¹¹ Calling a ravenous bird from the east, the man that executeth my counsel from a far country: yea, I have spoken *it*, I will also bring it to pass; I have purposed *it*, I will also do it. ¹² Hearken unto me, ye stouthearted, that *are* far from righteousness: ¹³ I bring near my righteousness; it shall not be far off, and my salvation shall not tarry: and I will place salvation in Zion for Israel my glory" (Isaiah 46:5-13).

Does God Cause Sin or Evil?

Joseph is certainly a good example of how God's instrumentation and orchestration brought good results out of a bad situation. The extreme Calvinist would say God decreed the sin of Joseph's brothers when they sold him into slavery.

In other words, God *caused* the sin to bring about the outcomes that He wanted. **This is a blasphemous proposition.** Secondly, and most importantly, this is not what the Scriptures say regarding this.

"[15] And when Joseph's brethren saw that their father was dead, they said, Joseph will peradventure hate us, and will certainly requite us all **the evil which we did unto him**. [16] And they sent a messenger unto Joseph, saying, Thy father did command before he died, saying, [17] So shall ye say unto Joseph, Forgive, I pray thee now, **the trespass of thy brethren, and their sin**; for they did unto thee evil: and now, we pray thee, forgive the trespass of the servants of the God of thy father. And Joseph wept when they spake unto him. [18] And his brethren also went and fell down before his face; and they said, Behold, we *be* thy servants. [19] And Joseph said unto them, Fear not: for *am* I in the place of God? [20] But as for you, **ye thought evil against me;** *but* **God meant it unto good, to bring to pass, as** *it is* **this day, to save much people alive**. [21] Now therefore fear ye not: I will nourish you, and your little ones. And he comforted them, and spake kindly unto them" (Genesis 50:15-21).

God is never the cause of sin. God does not even *tempt* with sin (James 1:13). Simply because God foreknows the outcomes and is able through His omnipotence, omniscience, and omnipresence to instrument and orchestrate good results out of sinful actions does not mean He *caused* those sinful actions in any way. The idea that God causes sin is a manifestation of a very low view of God, His holiness, and His sovereignty. However, God can work good out of the consequences of sinful actions. In fact, He promises He will do that for "them that love" Him.

"[26] Likewise the Spirit also **helpeth our infirmities**: for we know not what we should pray for as we ought: but the Spirit itself maketh intercession for us with groanings which cannot be uttered. [27] And he that searcheth the hearts knoweth what *is* the mind of the Spirit, because he maketh intercession for the saints according to *the will of* God. [28] And **we know that all things work together for good to them that love God, to them who are the** {*vocationally*} **called according to *his* purpose**" (Romans 8:26-28).

Acts of sin, either our own or the sin of others in our immediate association, can bring us into horrendous and seemingly hopeless situations due to the natural consequences of sin or the supernatural chastisement of God. The great truth of God's *omni-influence* is that He never leaves His redeemed alone merely to fend for themselves in the human predicament of sin.   God is always with them intimately and immediately working "all things . . . together for good . . . according to *his* purpose."   This is what defines God's sovereignty. A.T. Robertson comments on the meaning of Romans 8:26:

"Here beautifully Paul pictures the Holy Spirit taking hold at our side at the very time of our weakness (associative instrumental case) and before too late."[29]

Amos 3:6 is a text quoted by extreme Calvinists to support their idea that God *causes* "evil."   They do this knowing they take this verse completely out of the context of God's chastisement upon the children of Israel for their sin. There is an "evil" which is immoral sin. **God does not do this.** There is also an "evil," which is the consequences of sin,

---

[29] A. T. Robertson, *Word Pictures in the New Testament, Volume IV*, The Epistles of Paul, Baker Book House, Grand Rapids, Mich., page 376.

i.e., unpleasant, and hurtful results of chastisement. **God
allows this. It is to this latter that Amos 3:6 speaks.**

"[1] Hear this word that the LORD hath spoken against
you, O children of Israel, against the whole family
which I brought up from the land of Egypt, saying, [2]
You only have I known of all the families of the earth:
therefore I will punish you for all your iniquities. [3] **Can
two walk together, except they be agreed?** [4] Will a
lion roar in the forest, when he hath no prey? will a
young lion cry out of his den, if he have taken nothing?
[5] Can a bird fall in a snare upon the earth, where no gin
is for him? shall *one* take up a snare from the earth, and
have taken nothing at all? [6] Shall a trumpet be blown in
the city, and the people not be afraid? **shall there be evil
in a city, and the LORD hath not done *it*"** (Amos 3:1-
6)?

E. B. Pusey quotes Augustine on Amos 3:6.

"Is there evil in the city and the Lord hath not done it? -
Evil is of two sorts, evil of sin, and evil of punishment.
There is no other; for evil of nature, or evil of fortune,
are evils, by God's Providence, punishing the evil of sin.
Augustine, c. Adim. 26: '**Evil, which is sin, the Lord
hath not done; evil, which is punishment for sin, the
Lord bringeth.'** The Providence of God governing and
controlling all things, man doth ill which he wills, so as
to suffer ill which he wills not. Only, evil which is by
God's Providence the punishment of sin is in this life

remedial and through final impenitence alone becomes purely judicial."[30] (Bolding added for accent.)

Did God create beings that became evil? Yes, everything that exists came from God's creative acts. **However, God did not create evil beings.** Evil beings became evil because they chose to oppose God's order. God gave dominion of all His creation, including angels, to Adam. In God's order, angels became the servants of man. Some angels rebelled against that sovereign order and began to oppose God's sovereign order by seeking to destroy mankind. These fallen angels would seek to accomplish their purpose by tempting and influencing man to sin and thereby bring God's judgment upon sin. God restrains the operations of fallen angels through the omni-influence of His Spirit and "in wrath remember[s] mercy" (Habakkuk 3:2).

God's judgment upon nations and His chastisement upon His children are accomplished by merely removing His restraint by degrees upon the destructive forces of evil. This is what we find in the book of Revelation during the time referred to as the *Tribulation*. As God removes His restraint upon evil by degrees, the destructive forces of evil will be released more and more into the world causing more and more destruction. **God does not cause the evil.** He simply removes His restraint upon the evil that already exists (as an act of justice/judgment and wrath).

Another area of confusion regarding God's sovereignty is the doctrine of *ordination*. The word translated "ordain" in the Old Testament Scriptures is the Hebrew word *`asah* (aw-saw'). It is used in a very broad sense throughout the Old Testament Scriptures. It is used of things men *ordain*

---

[30] E. B. Pusey, *Albert Barnes' Notes on the Old & New Testaments, Minor Prophets, Vol. I*, Baker Book House, Grand Rapids, Mich., page 273.

and it is used of things God *ordains*. It is used of things God creates ("made," Genesis 1:7, 16, 25, 26, 31, 2:2, 3, 4; etc.) and of what the thing made produces ("yielding," Gen. 1:11-12). It is used of the things man does (Genesis 3:13). It is even used of things Satan does (Genesis 3:14). The ***Theological Workbook of the Old Testament*** provides some interesting insight into the use of this word.

> "When used of God, the word frequently emphasizes God's acts in the sphere of history. These contexts stress one of the most basic concepts of OT theology, i.e., that God is not only transcendent, but he is also immanent in history, effecting his sovereign purpose. Moses could recall God's great acts in Egypt, reminding the people of all that God 'did' (Deut. 29:1). That which God has done to the nations is a testimony to God's intervention in history (Josh 23:3). Solomon, in his dedicatory prayer, could beseech God to 'act' (I Kgs 8:39). The word *'asah* is often used of signs and wonders performed by God in the course of history (Joh 24:17; Psalm 98:1; Isa 25:1), demonstrating again the heavy emphasis in the OT on the immanence of God."[31]

A critical error of both Calvinism and Arminianism is that they equate God's predestination with God's election in the supposition that God has chosen certain individuals to be saved from eternal condemnation. They like to quote Acts 13:48 to *proof text* this point of their theology, when in fact this text does not mean what they say it means at all. "And when the Gentiles

---

[31] R. Laird Harris, Gleason L. Archer, Jr., Bruce K. Waltke, *Theological Workbook of the Old Testament, Vol. II*, Moody Press, Chicago, IL, page 701.

heard this, they were glad, and glorified the word of the Lord: and as many as **were ordained to eternal life believed**."

Henry Alford makes a detailed explanation of Acts 13:48 contradicting the suppositions of Calvinism imposed upon this text.

"The meaning of [tetagmenoi] must be determined by the context. The Jews had *judged themselves unworthy of eternal life*: the Gentiles, **as many as were disposed to eternal life**, believed. *By whom* so disposed, is not *here* declared: nor need the word be in this place further particularized. *We know that it is God who worketh in us the will to believe*, and that the preparation of the heart is of Him: but **to find in *this text* pre-ordination to life asserted, is to force both the word and the context to a meaning which they do not contain.** The key to the word here is the comparison of ref. [I Cor. 16:15 and Rom. 13:1] in both of which places the *agents* are expressed, whereas here the word is absolute. See also ch. xx.13..."[32] [English alphabetizing of the Greek replaced.]

The most critical argument *against* the abuse of God's sovereignty espoused by *particular election* or by God's *foreordination of particular individuals to eternal life* is God's Word itself. **It is blasphemy for Calvinism to create a god that is contrary to the declarations of Who He is in the Word of God.**

"[1] I exhort therefore, that, first of all, supplications, prayers, intercessions, *and* giving of thanks, be made for **all men**; [2] For kings, and *for* all that are in authority; that

---

[32] Henry Alford, *Alford's Greek New Testament, Vol. II*, Baker Book House, Grand Rapids, Mich., page 153.

we may lead a quiet and peaceable life in all godliness and honesty. [3] For this *is* good and acceptable in the sight of God our Saviour; [4] **Who will have all men to be saved**, and to come unto the knowledge of the truth. [5] For *there is* one God, and one mediator between God and men, the man Christ Jesus; [6] **Who gave himself a ransom for all**, to be testified in due time" (I Timothy 2:1-6).

"The Lord is not slack concerning his promise, as some men count slackness; but is longsuffering to us-ward, **not willing that any should perish, but that all should come to repentance**" (II Peter 3:9).

"[11] For the grace of God that bringeth salvation **hath appeared to all men**, [12] Teaching us that, denying ungodliness and worldly lusts, we should live soberly, righteously, and godly, in this present world; [13] Looking for that blessed hope, and the glorious appearing of the great God and our Saviour Jesus Christ; [14] Who gave himself for us, that he might redeem us from all iniquity, and purify unto himself a peculiar people, zealous of good works" (Titus 2:11-14).

The Poisoned Tulip

The Corporate/Vocational View of Election
Chapter Five
Blasphemy of Limited Atonement and Irresistible Grace

Having conclusively and scripturally shown that nowhere in Scripture does God say that He has elected *particular people* **to be regenerated so that they can believe, we can go on and deal with the falsehoods of** *limited atonement* **and** *irresistible grace.*

First, election is *vocational,* **not** *salvational,* **according to God's ordained purposes.** Secondly, election is primarily corporate in scope, i.e., the nation of Israel and then the Church as a new priesthood. Thirdly, God choses individuals for His divine purposes (prophets, judges, kings, and priests) and many of these individuals are never "born again" (pharaoh, Judas, etc.). Therefore, the *theological domino* of *irresistible grace* automatically falls with the falsehood of *unconditional election.*

It has also been conclusively shown that the *total depravity* **as being taught by Calvinists as** *total inability* **is not scripturally viable. Humans can still make moral choices even when they are "dead in trespasses and sins" (Ephesians 2:1).**

Professing Christians have become so accustomed to using the terminology of Reformed Theology, they do not even think to ask if the terminology is scriptural. Must of the terminology of Reformed Theology is unscriptural.

Whosoever Shall Call . . . Shall be Saved!

"[11] For the scripture saith, **Whosoever believeth** on him shall not be ashamed. [12] For there is no difference between the Jew and the Greek: for the same Lord over all is rich unto all that call upon him. [13] For **whosoever**

shall call upon the name of the Lord shall be saved"
(Romans 10:11-13).

The *contextual continuity* of the epistle to the Romans
demands that we see Romans chapter ten in the *light* of three
dominant truths already established from the earlier chapters:

1. God is *universally* propitiated for the sins of the whole
world from the Fall to the end of time. Sinners must
understand this and *believe this*.
2. This translates into *universal provision* of the gift of
justification (the righteousness of Christ imparted to the
believing sinner, II Peter 1:4) to "whoever shall call upon
the Name of the LORD." Justification is available to
"whosoever." Sinners must *understand* this and *believe
this*.
3. Although both of these two statements are true and
should be universally applied, and although Christ's death,
burial, and resurrection is **sufficient for the salvation of
all**, it is **beneficial only to those who respond in faith
according to God's inspired directives.** These directives
include repentance from sin and "dead works." These
directives include understanding and believing the
objective facts of the finished work of redemption as
detailed in the Gospel of Jesus Christ. These directives
include confessing Jesus to be Jehovah incarnate and
calling on the Name of Jesus as Jehovah to save. These
directives include receiving Jesus Christ in the indwelling
of the Holy Spirit of God.
No one would have a problem following the
***contextual continuity* of the epistle to the Romans and the
categorical theological establishment of the three
statements above if it were not for the presuppositions of
Calvinism and Reformed Theology that are imposed upon
the epistle.** For Calvinists, the word "whosoever" means

whosoever of the elect. For Calvinists, when God says it is His will that *all* come to repentance and that *all* are saved, it means *all who are elect.* For Calvinists, God's love for the world refers to two distinct kinds of grace. This is a blasphemous misrepresentation of the grace of God and of the character and nature of God.

Understanding *Manufactured Theological Terms* that Distort God's Grace

1. Common Grace (or *Prevenient Grace*) comes to all people. This is basically defined as God temporally withholding His judgment upon sinners and the *reprobate* (those not chosen by God to be saved), allowing them the *common blessings* of life ("the rain falls on the just and the unjust alike").

2. Irresistible Grace (*Efficacious Grace*) comes only to the *elect* (those chosen by God to be saved). They believe God *regenerates* only the *elect* at some unknown time before their salvation, giving them the *gift* of repentance and faith in the indwelling of the Person of the Holy Spirit. In this pre-salvation regeneration, the *elect* sinner will not be able to *resist* God's grace and will at some unknown time in his/her life place faith in Jesus Christ. Because of this *special* working of God in the lives of the *elect* person, he/she will ultimately *persevere* in the Christian life proving he/she is one of God's *elect* (this is not the same as the Bible doctrine of *eternal security*).

These two distorted views of God's grace flow from three other theological *presuppositional* aberrations of Calvinism and Reformed Theology imposed upon the interpretation of the whole Word of God.

1. Monothetism: the monothetic definition of God's sovereignty (whatever God wills to be done must ALWAYS be done or realized).

2. Determinism: God is the ultimate cause of all things thereby *controlling* all events in human history and in the future. God can *foretell* the future, not just because of *foreknowledge*, because God *controls* and *causes* all events in history.

3. Monergism: being saved is not based upon the will of an individual making a faith decision to trust Christ, but upon the *sovereign will* of God operating *within,* not *upon*, the *elect* prior to their salvation by regenerating them before salvation so that they can believe.

In Calvin's preface to his ***Institutes of the Christian Religion*** (second edition of 1539), we have a defining statement that really tells us why the *exegesis* of all Calvinists is perverted, transforming it into *eisegesis*. This happens because all Calvinists look at the Scriptures through the *theological presuppositions* of Calvin. This is clearly stated as Calvin's *purpose* in writing his ***Institutes of the Christian Religion.***

"I have endeavored to give such a summary of religion in all its parts (*in the systemic theology laid out in his Institutes of the Christian Religion*), and have digested it into such an order as may make it not difficult for anyone who is rightly acquainted with it (*the systemic theology laid out in his Institutes of the Christian Religion*) to ascertain both what he ought principally **to look for** in Scripture, and also to what head he ought to refer whatever is contained in it. Having thus, as it were, paved the way, I shall not feel it necessary in any Commentaries on Scripture which I may afterwards publish to enter into long discussions of doctrine or dilate on commonplaces, and will therefore always compress them. In this way the pious reader will be saved much trouble and weariness, provided he comes furnished with a knowledge of the present work (*the systemic theology laid out in his Institutes of the Christian Religion*) as an **essential prerequisite**."[33] (bolding and parenthesized areas added)

What does this statement of Calvin tell us? This prefacing statement of Calvin's Institutes of Religion is a definitive reality behind most of what defines the *hermeneutics* of Calvinism and Reformed Theology. Calvin made his *Institutes of the Christian Religion* "an essential prerequisite" to being able to *properly exegete the Scriptures accurately*. **In doing so, Calvin has also negatively transformed the Biblical interpretation (hermeneutics) of every Calvinist (anyone believing the theology of his *Institutes of the Christian Religion*) into *eisegesis*.**

Returning to the *contextual continuity* of the epistle to Romans chapter ten, let us inductively examine from other Scriptures the three dominant truths we have mentioned.

1. God is *universally* propitiated for the sins of the entire world from the fall to the end of time.

Most Calvinists define propitiation as the *appeasement* of God's wrath upon sin, rather than the *satisfaction* of God's wrath. The word *appease,* as used in this manner, is like eating an apple to *satisfy* your hunger. There is a degree of satisfaction, but it is temporary or momentary until hunger arises once again. This is the way the pagans

---

[33] As quoted by Robert Shank, *Elect in the Son, A Study of the Doctrine of Election,* Bethany House Publishers, Minneapolis, MN, 1970, pages 227-228.

viewed *appeasing* their idolatrous *gods*. **This in no way reflects the accurate meaning of propitiation as used in the Word of God. In the Word of God there is a *once for all* satisfaction of God's wrath upon sin in the death, burial, and resurrection of His sinless Son.** In the sense of the Biblical usage of the word propitiation, it is clearly a term used in the sense of **complete adjudication of divine sentence intent upon remission of the penalty** upon the sinner by mitigating the sentence in the death of a substitute. "It is finished."

"[20] Therefore by the deeds of the law there shall no flesh be justified in his sight: for by the law *is* the knowledge of sin. [21] But now the righteousness of God without the law is manifested, being witnessed by the law and the prophets; [22] Even **the righteousness of God *which is* by faith of Jesus Christ unto all and upon all them that believe**: for there is no difference: [23] For all have sinned, and come short of the glory of God; [24] **Being justified freely by his grace through the redemption that is in Christ Jesus**: [25] Whom God hath set forth *to be* a propitiation through faith in his blood, to declare his righteousness **for the remission of sins** that are past, through the forbearance of God; [26] To declare, *I say*, at this time his righteousness: **that he might be just, and the justifier of him which believeth in Jesus**" (Romans 3:20-26).

The word translated "remission" in Romans 3:25 is the Greek word *paresis* (par'-es-is), which means "passing over." It refers to God's *passing over* or *covering over* sin in the Old Testament sense until the coming of Messiah and the *finished work* of Calvary. This is the only use of this word in the New Testament books of the Bible, and it refers to what was done in the Old Covenant economy. Because Calvinists and

Reformed Theologians, in most part, do not understand dispensation transitions, they do not understand the difference between the sacrifice of the *Kaphar* (Atonement) offering of the Mosaic Covenant, which only *covered over* sins, and the sacrifice of Christ, which completely, *once for all*, pays for and removes the penalty of sin upon the *believing* sinner (Romans 6:23). **Believing** (Romans 10:9, *resting in the truth*) is the *condition* for a sinner to vocationally *become* one of the elect "in Christ" in the priesthood of all believers.

Understanding the Universal Propitiation of God's Wrath Destroys Limited Atonement

Clearly, the word propitiation in the Word of God is used in the context of *jurisprudence*. In other words, it is a word used to describe *divine justice*. A *just judge* cannot be just if he does not require the sentence that he places upon the guilty to be executed exactly as he demands. God cannot merely forgive the debt of the transgression of sin. **God must satisfy the debt by taking the sentence upon Himself substitutionally by becoming a man, living a sinless life, and dying in the place of sinners.** The advocacy of Jesus before the eternal Father is pleading the case of redemption on behalf of those "born again" "by grace through faith" in His finished, vicarious work of redemption.

"[1] My little children, these things write I unto you, that ye sin not. And if any man sin, **we have an advocate with the Father**, Jesus Christ the righteous: [2] And **he is the propitiation for our sins: and not for ours only, but also for *the sins of* the whole world**" (I John 2:1-2).

To take the substitutionary death of Jesus out of the context of the *universal propitiation* of God for the sins of the whole world from the fall to the end of time would completely distort the intent of God in the incarnation of Christ, His sinless life, and the purpose of His substitutionary death on the Cross of Calvary. **Calvinists corrupt *universal propitiation* when they teach *Limited Atonement*.** As the believer's advocate, Jesus stands before the Father and proclaims the sinner "in Christ" to be free from condemnation (Romans 8:1) and perfectly righteous in the substitute. This *once for all* aspect of the propitiation of God is thoroughly declared and exemplified in Hebrews chapter ten.

"[7] Then said I, Lo, I come (in the volume of the book it is written of me,) to do thy will, O God. [8] Above when he said, Sacrifice and offering and burnt offerings and *offering* for sin thou wouldest not, neither hadst pleasure *therein*; which are offered by the law; [9] Then said he, Lo, I come to do thy will, O God. He taketh away the first, that he may establish the second. [10] **By the which will we are sanctified through the offering of the body of Jesus Christ once *for all*.** [11] And every priest standeth daily ministering and offering oftentimes the same sacrifices, which can never take away sins: [12] But this man, after he had offered **one sacrifice for sins for ever**, sat down on the right hand of God; [13] From henceforth expecting till his enemies be made his footstool. [14] For **by one offering he hath perfected for ever them that are sanctified**. [15] *Whereof* the Holy Ghost also is a witness to us: for after that he had said before, [16] This *is* the covenant that I will make with them after those days, saith the Lord, I will put my laws into their hearts, and in their minds will I write them; [17] And their sins and iniquities will I remember no more. [18] **Now where remission of these *is*, there *is* no more offering for sin**" (Hebrews 10:7-18).

Calvinists take the word *atonement*, used only once in the New Testament in Romans 5:11 where it should be translated "reconciliation," and use the word *atonement* like it was used in the Old Testament. **In the Mosaic Covenant, the sacrifices cried out to God for complete propitiation.**

Thereby, Calvinists can make the ordinances of water baptism and the Lord's Supper sacramental through which grace is conferred to participants. This is a complete contradiction of the word *atonement* created by William Tyndale in his English translation of the Bible. Tyndale created this word and translated it as At-One-Ment.

2. *Universal propitiation* translates into *universal provision* of the *gift* of salvation to "whoever shall call upon the Name of the LORD." Salvation is available to "whosoever."

To whom was the *universal propitiation* of God provided? *Universal propitiation* is nonsensical apart from the nature and scope of *universal provision.* On other words, although God is the One propitiated, the benefit of propitiation is *for* sinners (Romans 3:36). Therefore, the very idea of *limited atonement* is nonsensical considering the overwhelming Scriptural evidence to the contrary.

"[7] Thou madest him a little lower than the angels; thou crownedst him with glory and honour, and didst set him over the works of thy hands: [8] Thou hast put all things in subjection under his feet. For in that he put all in subjection under him, he left nothing *that is* not put under him. But now we see not yet all things put under him. [9] But we see Jesus, who was made a little lower than the angels for the suffering of death, crowned with glory and honour; **that he by the grace of God should taste death for every man**" (Hebrews 2:7-9).

"[3] For this *is* good and acceptable in the sight of God our Saviour; [4] **Who will have all men to be saved**, and to come unto the knowledge of the truth. [5] For *there is* one God, and one mediator between God and men, the man Christ Jesus; ⁶ **Who gave himself a ransom <u>for</u> <u>all</u>**, to be testified in due time" (I Timothy 2:3-6).

Apart from the *universal provision* of salvation to "whosoever," the *universal propitiation* of God does not fully define the universal love of God for fallen and lost sinners. Therefore, *limited atonement* distorts both the grace of God and the universal expression of that grace in the love of God for sinners through the substitutionary death of Jesus the Christ, which is the primary purpose for which the Son of God was incarnated. **The *sovereign grace* teaching that Jesus died only for the *elect* is blasphemy.**

"¹⁴ And as Moses lifted up the serpent in the wilderness, even so must the Son of man be lifted up: ¹⁵ That **whosoever believeth** in him should not perish, but have eternal life. ¹⁶ For God so loved the world, that he gave his only begotten Son, **that whosoever believeth** in him should not perish, but have everlasting life. ¹⁷ For God sent not his Son into the world to condemn the world; but that the world through him might be saved. ¹⁸ **He that believeth** on him is not condemned: but he that believeth not is condemned already, because he hath not believed in the name of the only begotten Son of God" (John 3:14-18).

The fact that the *universal propitiation* of God is intended for *universal provision* of salvation to "whosoever" is exemplified by Peter's statement in his second epistle. Peter is exposing false teachers who had rejected the Gospel of Jesus and were mocking the possibility of His second coming. Christ's redemptive propitiation is *sufficient* and *efficacious* for all willing to believe "through faith" including those that denied Him.

"But there were false prophets also among the people, even as there shall be false teachers among you, who privily shall bring in damnable heresies, even **denying the Lord that bought them**, and bring upon themselves swift destruction" (II Peter 2:1).

The *Jamieson-Fausset-Brown Commentary* says, "**bought them**--Even the ungodly were bought by His 'precious blood.' It shall be their bitterest self-reproach in hell, that, as far as Christ's redemption was concerned, they might have been saved. The denial of His *propitiatory* sacrifice is included in the meaning (compare 1John 4:3)."[34] **Clearly, the universal propitiation of God is intended to universally provide salvation to "whosoever."**

3. Although both of the previous two statements are true and should be universally applied, and although Christ's death, burial, and resurrection is *sufficient* for the salvation of all, **it is *efficacious* only to those who respond in faith. They must respond according to God's inspired directives of repentance from sin and "dead works," believing the objective facts of the finished work of redemption as detailed in the Gospel of Jesus Christ. They must also confess Jesus as Jehovah, calling on the Name of Jesus as Jehovah to save. Then they must receive Jesus Christ in the indwelling of the Holy Spirit of God.**

**Calvinist's Accusation of Universalism
Arguing Against Universal Propitiation**

"[6] For when we were yet without strength, in due time **Christ died for the ungodly**. [7] For scarcely for a

---

[34] Jamieson-Fausset-Brown Commentary, Sword Searcher Software, 4.8

righteous man will one die: yet peradventure for a good man some would even dare to die. [8] But God commendeth **his love toward us**, in that, while we were yet sinners, Christ died for us. [9] Much more then, being now justified by his blood, we shall be saved from wrath through him. [10] For if, when we were enemies, we were reconciled to God by the death of his Son, much more, being reconciled, we shall be saved by his life. [11] And not only *so*, but we also joy in God through our Lord Jesus Christ, by whom we **have now received the atonement** {*better translated reconciliation*}. [12] Wherefore, as by one man sin entered into the world, and death by sin; and so death passed upon all men, for that all have sinned: [13] (For until the law sin was in the world: but sin is not imputed when there is no law. [14] Nevertheless death reigned from Adam to Moses, even over them that had not sinned after the similitude of Adam's transgression, who is the figure of him that was to come. [15] But not as the offence, **so also *is* the free gift**. For if through the offence of one many be dead, much more the grace of God, and the gift by grace, *which is* by one man, Jesus Christ, **hath abounded unto many** {*sufficient for all but efficacious only to those that believe*}. [16] And not as *it was* by one that sinned, *so is* the gift: for the judgment *was* by one to condemnation, but the free gift *is* of many offences unto justification. [17] For if by one man's offence death reigned by one; much more they which receive abundance of grace and of the gift of righteousness shall reign in life by one, Jesus Christ.) [18] Therefore as by the offence of one *judgment came* upon all men to condemnation; **even so by the righteousness of one *the free gift came* upon all men unto** {*availability in universal provision*} **justification of life**. [19] For as by one man's disobedience many were made sinners, **so by**

the obedience of one shall many {*sufficient for all, but efficacious only to those that believe*} be made righteous" (Romans 5:6-19).

Because of Calvinists' *Monergism* (as Calvinists teach that God regenerates those He has elected to be saved before they believe), Calvinists demand that *universal propitiation* must therefore translate into universalism (*universal salvation*). If Christ died for the sins of the whole world (rather than just for the sins of the elect) then the whole world will be saved. Of course, this is mere nonsense. **Clearly the Word of God necessitates a response to the *universal provision*. A Biblically defined faith response is the *appropriation* of God's *universal provision*.** This response is communicated by the Biblical terms *believe* and *faith*. That is why the word "many" is used in Romans 5:15 and 19. **The *universal propitiation* of God results in the *universal provision* of the gift of salvation to "whosoever," but it does not result in the *universal salvation* of all sinners automatically. The *condition* of appropriation is *faith*.**

This very idea of *universal provision* to "whosoever" is an *abomination* to most Calvinists. Therefore, the word "whosoever" appears to be a dirty word for many in the *systemic theological* circles of Reformed Theology. This is apparent because they appear to be constantly trying to narrow its parameters of inclusion or redefine it altogether. Clearly the promises of the Abrahamic Covenant were intended to extend beyond the physical descendants of Abraham to "whosoever." Clearly this is *inclusivistic* terminology, not *exclusive* terminology.

Clearly from the context of Romans chapters nine and ten, the Holy Spirit's inspired choice of the word "whosoever" is intended to be a summary word that connects all "born again" people from all nations of the world to the eternal promises of God within the

Abrahamic Covenant. This is a truth constantly repeated in God's progressive history with Abraham.

"[1] Now the LORD had said unto Abram, Get thee out of thy country, and from thy kindred, and from thy father's house, unto a land that I will shew thee: [2] And I will make of thee a great nation, and I will bless thee, and make thy name great; and thou shalt be a blessing: [3] And I will bless them that bless thee, and curse him that curseth thee: **and in thee shall all families of the earth be blessed**" (Genesis 12:1-3).

"[13] And the LORD said unto Abraham, Wherefore did Sarah laugh, saying, Shall I of a surety bear a child, which am old? [14] Is any thing too hard for the LORD? At the time appointed I will return unto thee, according to the time of life, and Sarah shall have a son. [15] Then Sarah denied, saying, I laughed not; for she was afraid. And he said, Nay; but thou didst laugh. [16] And the men rose up from thence, and looked toward Sodom: and Abraham went with them to bring them on the way. [17] And the LORD said, Shall I hide from Abraham that thing which I do; [18] Seeing that Abraham shall surely become a great and mighty nation, **and all the nations of the earth shall be blessed in him**" (Genesis 18:13-18)?

"[15] And the angel of the LORD called unto Abraham out of heaven the second time, [16] And said, By myself have I sworn, saith the LORD, for because thou hast done this thing, and hast not withheld thy son, thine only *son*: [17] That in blessing I will bless thee, and in multiplying I will multiply thy seed as the stars of the heaven, and as the sand which *is* upon the sea shore; and thy seed shall possess the gate of his enemies; [18] **And in thy seed shall**

all the nations of the earth be blessed; because thou hast obeyed my voice" (Genesis 22:15-18).

"[1] And there was a famine in the land, beside the first famine that was in the days of Abraham. And Isaac went unto Abimelech king of the Philistines unto Gerar. [2] And the LORD appeared unto him, and said, Go not down into Egypt; dwell in the land which I shall tell thee of: [3] Sojourn in this land, and I will be with thee, and will bless thee; for unto thee, and unto thy seed, I will give all these countries, and I will perform the oath which I sware unto Abraham thy father; [4] And I will make thy seed to multiply as the stars of heaven, and will give unto thy seed all these countries; **and in thy seed shall all the nations of the earth be blessed**; [5] Because that Abraham obeyed my voice, and kept my charge, my commandments, my statutes, and my laws" (Genesis 26:1-5).

Obviously, the intent of the word "whosoever" comes with the intent of *universal application* to anyone wanting to be saved. In simple words, salvation is *universally available* to "whosoever shall call upon the name of the Lord" (Romans 10:13). There are no Jewish *boundaries* or *ethnic limitations* upon the *universal availability* of God's gift of salvation. The only exclusion that can possibly be applied here is to those unwilling to respond to the Gospel of Jesus Christ by an action of faith in repenting of sin and believing what the objective facts of Gospel accomplish for sinners. They are unwilling to confess Jesus to be Jehovah. They need not and do not call on the name of Jesus to save them from their helpless and desperate situation. Therefore, they never receive Jesus Christ as Lord and His imparted righteousness in the Person of the indwelling Holy Spirit, thereby being regenerated.

The inclusive intent of "whosoever" is also very much a part of God's dispensational transition in the progressive unfolding of the Abrahamic Covenant from the Mosaic Covenant into the New Covenant in Christ's Blood. This "whosoever" aspect of this transition into the New Covenant from the Mosaic Covenant was specifically revealed in the prophecy of Joel.

"[28] And it shall come to pass afterward, *that* I will pour out my spirit upon all flesh; and your sons and your daughters shall prophesy, your old men shall dream dreams, your young men shall see visions: [29] And also upon the servants and upon the handmaids in those days will I pour out my spirit. [30] And I will shew wonders in the heavens and in the earth, blood, and fire, and pillars of smoke. [31] The sun shall be turned into darkness, and the moon into blood, before the great and the terrible day of the LORD come. [32] And it shall come to pass, *that* **whosoever shall call on the name of the LORD shall be delivered**: for in mount Zion and in Jerusalem shall be deliverance, as the LORD hath said, and in the remnant whom the LORD shall call" (Joel 2:28-32).

Undoubtedly, the primary focus of the prophecy of Joel 2:28-32 has to do with the Tribulation period ("the terrible day of the LORD") between the Rapture of the Church and the second coming of Messiah. The message of the prophecy is not merely to Israel or national Jews living at that "terrible day," but to all people groups, cultures, ethnicities, and/or language groups. People from *any* of these groups could *call upon the name of Jehovah* in faith to be "delivered" from the terrible judgment of God upon the nations of the world. Although *all nations* inclusivistically would be judged, any *individual* from any of those nations ("whosoever") could cry out to Jehovah in faith to be delivered.

Both the Apostle Peter in Acts two and the Apostle Paul in Romans ten are quoting from the text in Joel two and are giving us a *complimentary hermeneutic* regarding how this text is to be understood through dispensational transitions. Peter's statements in Acts chapter two and Paul's statements in Romans chapter ten give us the perimeters of explanation in how the phrase "whosoever shall call on the name of the LORD shall be delivered" is practically expressed through faith in Jesus Christ and the accomplishments of the objective facts of the Gospel. Although there is some clarification and explanation of what it means to "call on the name of the LORD," the "whosoever" remains to be an *inclusive term.*

"¹⁴ But Peter, standing up with the eleven, lifted up his voice, and said unto them, Ye men of Judaea, and all *ye* that dwell at Jerusalem, be this known unto you, and hearken to my words: ¹⁵ For these are not drunken, as ye suppose, seeing it is *but* the third hour of the day. ¹⁶ **But this is that which was spoken by the prophet Joel;** ¹⁷ And it shall come to pass in the last days, saith God, I will pour out of my Spirit upon all flesh: and your sons and your daughters shall prophesy, and your young men shall see visions, and your old men shall dream dreams: ¹⁸ And on my servants and on my handmaidens I will pour out in those days of my Spirit; and they shall prophesy: ¹⁹ And I will shew wonders in heaven above, and signs in the earth beneath; blood, and fire, and vapour of smoke: ²⁰ The sun shall be turned into darkness, and the moon into blood, *before that great and notable day of the Lord come:* ²¹ And it shall come to pass, *that* **whosoever shall call on the name of the Lord shall be saved.** ²² Ye men of Israel, hear these words; Jesus of Nazareth, a man approved of God among you by miracles and wonders and signs, which God did by him in the midst of you, as ye yourselves also know: [23] Him, being delivered by the determinate counsel and foreknowledge of God, ye have taken, and by wicked hands have crucified and slain: [24] Whom God hath raised up, having loosed the pains of death: because it was not possible that he should be holden of it. [25] For David speaketh concerning him, I foresaw the Lord always before my face, for he is on my right hand, that I should not be moved: [26] Therefore did my heart rejoice, and my tongue was glad; moreover also my flesh shall rest in hope: [27] Because thou wilt not leave my soul in hell, neither wilt thou suffer thine Holy One to see corruption. [28] Thou hast made known to me the ways of life; thou shalt make me full of joy with thy countenance. [29] Men *and* brethren, let me freely speak unto you of the patriarch David, that he is both dead and buried, and his sepulchre is with us unto this day. [30] Therefore being a prophet, and knowing that God had sworn with an oath to him, that of the fruit of his loins, according to the flesh, he would raise up Christ to sit on his throne; [31] He seeing this before spake of the resurrection of Christ, that his soul was not left in hell, neither his flesh did see corruption. [32] This Jesus hath God raised up, whereof we all are witnesses. [33] Therefore being by the right hand of God exalted, and having received of the Father the promise of the Holy Ghost, he hath shed forth this, which ye now see and hear. [34] For David is not ascended into the heavens: but he saith himself, The LORD said unto my Lord, Sit thou on my right hand, [35] Until I make thy foes thy footstool. [36] Therefore let all the house of Israel know assuredly, that God hath made that same Jesus, whom ye have crucified, both Lord and Christ" (Acts 2:14-36).

We should not allow anyone to take the context of Joel chapter two away from the "whosoever" of either Acts chapter two or Romans chapter ten. Although the prophecies of Joel are only partially fulfilled (*already, not yet*) in the transition into the Dispensation of the Church Age, portions of those prophecies are fulfilled. In Acts chapter two, Peter tells us that the issue of being filled with the Spirit and the miracle of speaking in tongues was a sign to the Jews of a *partial* fulfillment of the prophecies of Joel chapter two.

Much like Calvinists, the Jews thought they had an exclusive claim on God's grace. During the Dispensation of the Law and the Mosaic Covenant, we might go as far as to say the Jews did have that claim to some degree. "Salvation {*in the birth, life, death, burial, and resurrection of Jesus*} is of the Jews" (John 4:22). This was spoken to the Samaritan woman in the context of a radical change in God's operations within humanity.

"[19] The woman saith unto him, Sir, I perceive that thou art a prophet. [20] Our fathers worshipped in this mountain; and ye say, that in Jerusalem is the place where men ought to worship. [21] Jesus saith unto her, Woman, believe me, **the hour cometh**, when ye shall neither in this mountain, nor yet at Jerusalem, worship the Father. [22] Ye worship ye know not what: we know what we worship: for salvation is of the Jews. [23] **But the hour cometh, and now is, when the true worshippers shall worship the Father in spirit and in truth: for the Father seeketh such to worship him**. [24] God *is* a Spirit: and they that worship him must worship *him* in spirit and in truth. [25] The woman saith unto him, I know that Messias cometh, which is called Christ: when he is come, he will tell us all things. [26] Jesus saith unto her, I that speak unto thee am *he*" (John 4:19-26).

During the Dispensation of Law and under the Mosaic Covenant, worshipping God came through a very definitive set of God ordained rules, sacrifices, and special days. However, once the fulfillment of the Law was completed in Jesus Christ, the *door* into the regeneration (i.e., *glorification*) no longer came through the *Gospel in the Law*. Faith in Jesus and the objective facts of what He accomplished through His death, burial, and resurrection became the *door* into "the regeneration" to "whosever will." Ever since the completion of redemption in the life, death, burial, and resurrection of Jesus Christ, no one needs to become a Jewish proselyte to be saved. "Whosoever will" can be saved and delivered. This is the Gospel of the Church Age and the Gospel of the Kingdom.

"¹⁶ I Jesus have sent mine angel to testify unto you these things in the churches. I am the root and the offspring of David, *and* the bright and morning star. ¹⁷ And the Spirit and the bride say, Come. And let him that heareth say, Come. And let him that is athirst come. And **whosoever will**, let him take the water of life freely" (Revelation 22:16-17).

The Universal Propitiation of God for the Sins of the Whole World

"¹ My little children, these things write I unto you, that ye sin not. And if any man sin, we have an advocate with the Father, Jesus Christ the righteous: ² And he is the propitiation for our sins: and not for ours only, but also for *the sins of* the whole world" (I John 2:1-2).

Calvinists who reject *limited atonement* refer to themselves as *Four Point Calvinists*. The Dutch Reformed church and the Synod of Dort (1618– 1619) was led by Theodore Beza and other Calvinists *limited atonement*. The

Synod of Dort listed what came to be called "the five heads of Dort" in the acronym TULIP. The third point of the TULIP acronym was limited atonement. Since many believe Calvin did not teach this, those believing in limited atonement are called *Hyper-Calvinists*. However, most Calvinists are *Five Pointers* and believe in *limited atonement*. It seems clear that Calvin himself believed in limited atonement from his commentary on I John 2:2.

"**2** *And not for ours only* He added this for the sake of amplifying, in order that the faithful might be assured that the expiation made by Christ, extends to all {*only*} **who by faith embrace the gospel**.
Here a question may be raised, how have the sins of the whole world been expiated? **I pass by the dotages of the fanatics, who under this pretense extend salvation to all the reprobate, and therefore to Satan himself. Such a monstrous thing deserves no refutation. They who seek to avoid this absurdity, have said that Christ suffered sufficiently for the whole world, but efficiently only for the elect. This solution has commonly prevailed in the schools. Though then I allow that what has been said is true, yet I deny that it is suitable to this passage;** for the design of John was no other than to make this benefit common to the whole Church. Then **under the word *all* or whole, he does not include the reprobate, but designates those who should believe as well as those who were then scattered through various parts of the world.** For then is really made evident, as it is meet, the

grace of Christ, when it is declared to be the only true salvation of the world."[35]

I John 2:2 certainly declares the universal propitiation of God for "for *the sins of* the whole world." Calvin calls universal propitiation an "absurdity." Calvin also uses the word "expiated" to translate the Greek word *hilasmos* (hilasmós), which the King James translators translated "propitiation." Although *expiation* can be a dictionary definition of *hilasmos*, it is not a theological definition.

Theologically the word *hilasmos* ("propitiation") refers to the full, complete, and righteous satisfaction of God's wrath by the adjudication of the sin penalty (eternal separation from God) through the death of the Substitute. This is considerably different than the dictionary definition: "the act of expiating something: the act of extinguishing the guilt incurred by something."[36]

In Calvin's commentary on Hebrews, he gives a brief statement on Hebrews 10:10, but then completely skips commenting on Hebrews 10:12, 14, and 18. These last three verses certainly demand a complete propitiation of God, the satisfaction of His wrath, and the full remission of the sin penalty for all who repent of sin and trust in the Mosaic Covenant (this includes the condemnation of beliefs in both *Sacerdotalism* and *Sacramentalism*).

Why does Calvin skip these verses in his commentary on Hebrews ten? Isn't it obvious? He skips these three verses because they completely contradict the continual sacramental offering of Christ in his view of Holy Communion (*the Eucharist*) whether one believes in

---

[35] Calvin, John, *John Calvin's Verse Commentary*, Module file location: C:\Program Files\SwordSearcher\ Modules\Calvin.ss5cmty, Module file time: 7/31/2011 9:15:26 PM UTC.

[36] *Merriam Webster Online Dictionary*, https://www.merriam-webster.com/dictionary/expiation.

Transubstantiation (the literal and physical presence of Christ in the bread and wine) or *Consubstantiation* (the spiritual presence of Christ in the bread and wine. Hebrews 10:12, 14, and 18 teach the universal propitiation of God once for all forever through the one sacrifice of Jesus.

"[7] Then said I, Lo, I come (in the volume of the book it is written of me,) to do thy will, O God. [8] Above when he said, Sacrifice and offering and burnt offerings and *offering* for sin thou wouldest not, neither hadst pleasure *therein*; which are offered by the law; [9] Then said he, Lo, I come to do thy will, O God. **He taketh away the first** {*Mosaic Covenant of incompleteness*}**, that he may establish the second** {*the New Covenant in Christ's Blood and complete, once for all forever propitiation*}. [10] By the which will we are sanctified {*perfect, passive- referring to once for all forever positional sanctification*} through the offering of the body of Jesus Christ once *for all*. [11] And every {*Mosaic Covenant*} priest standeth daily ministering and offering oftentimes the same sacrifices, **which can never take away sins** {*the meaning is can never remit of penalty of sins*}: [12] But **this man** {*Jesus as Melchizedekian High Priest*}, after he had offered **one sacrifice for sins for ever**, sat down on the right hand of God; [13] From henceforth expecting till his enemies be made his footstool. [14] For by **one offering he hath perfected for ever** {*the efficacy of this singular propitiatory sacrifice of Jesus is eternal*} **them that are sanctified**. [15] *Whereof* the Holy Ghost also is a witness to us: for after that he had said before, [16] This *is* the covenant that I will make with them after those days, saith the Lord, I will put my laws into their hearts, and in their minds will I write them; [17] And **their sins and iniquities will I remember no more.** [18] Now **where**

remission of these *is, there is* no more offering for sin" (Hebrews 10:9-18).

Calvin's sacramental view of Holy Communion held the view that Christ spiritually, not physically, entered the elements of bread and wine and these *consubstantiated elements* became spiritual food for the elect and *only* the elect. Do not try to understand how he/they determine who were the elect and who were not, because it is circular argument of pure rationalism.

"I should like to know how the wicked can eat the flesh of Christ which was not crucified for them, and how they can drink the blood which was not shed to expiate their sins."[37]

Certainly, Calvin's misunderstanding of universal propitiation connects to his sacramental view of Holy Communion as a continual offering of the body and blood of Jesus as spiritual food and spiritual drink. With that type of misunderstanding of the ordinance of the Lord's Supper as a *sacrament* rather than a *memorial*, can he be trusted with his understanding of the once for all forever propitiation of God in the one offering of Jesus?

---

[37] Calvin, John in his written arguments with Heshusius, available in English transition online at: http://www.godrules.net/library/calvin/142calvin_b13.htm.

The Poisoned Tulip

The Corporate/Vocational View of Election
Chapter Six
Irresistible Grace

Irresistible grace (*efficacious grace*) is a Calvinist doctrine that teaches that saving grace is only *effectual* to those God choses to be saved and regenerates against their will or apart from the chosen one's knowledge. In this false doctrine of Calvinism's regeneration (*Monergism*), the one regenerated is given repentance, faith, and a *new heart* before he/she is saved. Once this person is regenerated, has this *new heart*, repentance, and faith, he/she will not be able to *resist* God's *gracious* call to believe the Gospel and will be saved. Calvinists believe that this *new heart* is the indwelling of the Spirit of God who then extends an *inward call* to those elected of which call the now regenerate cannot and will not resist. **It appears the Calvinists have this all logically worked out except for one small problem: none of this is found anywhere in Scripture. It is all made up!**

The word *grace* in the Bible is a word to describe all the undeserved good God is trying to do and is doing in this cursed creation to bring all sinners to salvation and to enable all believers to volitionally choose to live righteously. God's grace began before the "foundation of the world" in the provision of a planned Redeemer in anticipation of Adam's sin, the fall of humanity, and the necessity of a just God's curse upon the first creation and its fallen beings.

God's grace is His unmerited/undeserved favor extending to human beings first for their regeneration and salvation (Ephesians 2:8-9). Then, once "born again," God's extends His grace to believers to enable them to live sanctified lives before Him (Romans 8:28). Grace is everything and anything God does within fallen humanity cursed to eternal separation from God. Anything God does for anyone within the cursed creation is of God's grace, goodness, and love for no one deserves anything from God but condemnation (John 3:16).

Clearly Scripture details God's general gracious working in the lives of all sinners before salvation (John 3:16 and Romans 10:13). Secondly, Scripture clearly teaches a heighten and specific working of enabling grace in the lives of all believers after salvation, especially to those that love the Lord and serve Him in holiness (Romans 8:28).

Common or Prevenient Grace (preceding salvation)

Although God is *preeminent* (set apart from all other beings by His perfections), He is also *imminent* (actively present within His creation). The *imminence* of God refers to His omnipresence and influences of that presence within His creation. All God's *imminence* is undeserved and is a gift of God's wondrous grace. It is this *common grace* that protects all humans from immediate destruction by Satan and other fallen angels. This *common grace* might be called *restraining grace*. Secondly it is this *common grace* that reproves/convicts all humans "of sin, and of righteousness, and of judgment" (John 16:8), while drawing all unto to salvation (John 12:32). Isaiah 6:1-4 details both God's *preeminence* and His *imminence*.

"[1] In the year that king Uzziah died I saw also the Lord sitting upon a throne, **high and lifted** up, and his train filled the temple. [2] Above it stood the seraphims: each one had six wings; with twain he covered his face, and with twain he covered his feet, and with twain he did fly. [3] And one cried unto another, and said, **Holy, holy, holy, *is* the LORD of hosts: the whole earth *is* full of his glory**. [4] And the posts of the door moved at the voice

of him that cried, and the house was filled with smoke"
(Isaiah 6:1-4).

"9 The Lord is not slack concerning his promise
{*Genesis 3:15 and 12:3*}, as some men count slackness;
but is longsuffering to us-ward, **not willing that any
should perish, but that all should come to
repentance**" (II Peter 3:9).

**The Calvinist will vehemently object to any
teaching that God wants all people to be "born again" and
is drawing all sinners to Himself. Yet Jesus said, "if I be
lifted up from the earth, will draw all *men* unto me" in
John 12:32.** As we have already shown, the Calvinists'
vehement objection is because they believe God has only
chosen a few to be "born again" and because they believe
Jesus only propitiated God for those God choses to be saved.
Therefore, verses like John 12:32 must be explained away by
the Calvinists to satisfy their presupposed *closed systemic
theology*.

"27 Now is my soul troubled; and what shall I say?
Father, save me from this hour: but for this cause came
I unto this hour. 28 Father, glorify thy name. Then came
there a voice from heaven, *saying*, I have both glorified
it, and will glorify *it* again. 29 The people therefore, that
stood by, and heard *it*, said that it thundered: others said,
An angel spake to him. 30 Jesus answered and said, This
voice came not because of me, but for your sakes. 31
Now is the judgment of this world: now shall the prince
of this world be cast out. 32 And I, **if** {*condition*} **I be
lifted up from the earth** {*He was 'lifted up'*}**, will
draw all *men* unto me** {*He is drawing 'all men' to Him
and salvation*}" (John 12:27-32).

Saving Grace and Differentiating from the Error of *Sovereign Grace or Monergism*

Again, the basic meaning of the word grace in the context of salvation is God's undeserved/unmerited gift in receiving sinners "through faith" in the finished work of redemption. This gift is provided through the substitutionary offering of Jesus for the penalty of sin for all sinners. This grace is the operation of the Spirit of God Who brings sinners to understand the penalty of sin, the impossibility of self-righteousness through "works" or rituals, and to understand the universal propitiation of God by Jesus Christ's death. The Spirit also gives understanding that Jesus is Jehovah God incarnate as both the Son of God and the son of man, and that the one understanding all of this about Jesus must in absolute desperation call out to Jesus to save his/her wretched soul. This is available to "whosoever." This is all spelled out for us in detail in Romans 10:1-13.

"[1] Brethren, my heart's desire and prayer to God for Israel is, that they might be saved. [2] For I bear them record that they have a zeal of God, but not according to knowledge. [3] For they being ignorant of God's righteousness, and **going about to establish their own righteousness**, have not submitted themselves **unto the righteousness of God** {*justification offered by grace through faith*}. [4] For Christ *is* the end of the law for righteousness to every one that believeth. [5] For Moses describeth the righteousness which is of the law, That the man which doeth those things shall live by them. [6] But the righteousness which is of faith speaketh on this wise, Say not in thine heart, Who shall ascend into heaven? (that is, to bring Christ down *from above*:) [7] Or, Who shall descend into the deep? (that is, to bring up Christ again from the dead.) [8] But what saith it? The word is nigh thee, *even* in thy mouth, and in thy heart: that is, the word of faith, which we preach; [9] That if thou shalt confess with thy mouth the Lord Jesus, and shalt believe in thine heart that God hath raised him from the dead, thou shalt be saved. [10] For with the heart man believeth unto righteousness; and with the mouth confession is made unto salvation. [11] For the scripture saith, Whosoever believeth on him shall not be ashamed. [12] For there is no difference between the Jew and the Greek: for the same Lord over all is rich unto all that call upon him. [13] For whosoever shall call upon the name of the Lord shall be saved" (Romans 10:1-13).

Sanctifying Grace (grace enabling)

God's grace does not end with bringing a sinner to understand his/her condemnation and need of the Savior. God's grace continues in the believer's life through illumination of the Scriptures, conviction of sin, loving chastisement when we fail, and His inward enabling to live God's will through the filling of the indwelling Spirit. Once a sinner is "born again," that person is once for all forever positionally sanctified (Romans 5:1-2) by the gift of God-kind righteousness in the indwelling Holy Spirit. This *new standing* (position) "into this grace" defines God's constant inward operations of the Spirit of Christ, who seeks to live God's Will through the life of the fully yielded believer (Romans 6:11-13).

"[1] Therefore **being justified by faith**, we have peace with God through our Lord Jesus Christ: [2] **By whom also we have** {*perfect, active*} access by faith **into this grace wherein we stand** {*perfect, active*}, and rejoice in hope of the glory of God" (Romans 5:1-2).

However, God's *enabling grace* to live His will does not happen apart from the human will. The believer must yield his/her will to the Will of God in the Person of the indwelling Spirit of Christ. Then the indwelling Spirit of Christ will enable the fully surrendered believer to live God's will revealed through God's Word. This *partnership (synergism)* is called "fellowship" (I John 1:3-4) in the God's Word and is the result of the filling of the Spirit (Ephesians 5:18). All of this is part of God's *sanctifying work of grace* that *continues* throughout the temporal life of every "born again" believer. **This is NOT a *second work of grace.***

"[12] **Let not** {*matter of the will*} sin {*the fallen nature*} therefore reign in your mortal body, that ye should obey it in the lusts thereof. [13] **Neither yield** {*matter of the will*} ye your members *as* instruments of unrighteousness unto sin {*the fallen nature*}: but **yield yourselves unto God**, as those that are alive from the dead, and your members *as* instruments of righteousness unto God. [14] For sin {*the fallen nature*} shall not have dominion over you: for ye are not under the law, but under grace {*the supernatural enabling of the indwelling Spirit of God*}. [15] What then? shall we sin {*matter of the will*}, because we are not under the law, but under grace? God forbid. [16] Know ye not, that to **whom ye yield** {*matter of the will*} **yourselves servants to obey, his servants ye are to whom ye obey**; whether of sin {*the fallen nature*} unto death, or of obedience unto righteousness? [17] But God be thanked, that ye were the servants of sin {*the fallen nature*}, but **ye have obeyed from the heart** {*matter of the will*} that form of doctrine which was delivered you. [18] Being then made free from sin {*the fallen nature*}, **ye became the servants** {*matter of the will*} **of righteousness**" (Romans 6:12-18).

"[17] Wherefore be ye not unwise, but understanding what the will of the Lord *is*. [18] And be not drunk with wine, wherein is excess; but **be filled with the Spirit**;" (Ephesians 5:17-18).

"Be filled with the Spirit" is a present, passive, imperative, meaning it is a commandment. The passive voice means we cannot fill ourselves. We must simply yield to the indwelling Spirit with the intent of partnering with Him in doing God's will. When a believer is "filled with the Spirit" the effect of grace enabling affects and the *fruit of the Spirit* is released through that believer's life.

"[3] That which we have seen and heard declare we unto you, that ye also **may have fellowship with us**: and truly **our fellowship *is* with the Father, and with his Son Jesus Christ**. [4] And these things write we unto you, that your joy may be full. . . [7] But **if** {*condition*} we **walk in the light**{*cannot happen apart from yielding and being filled with the Spirit*}, **as he** is in the light, **we have fellowship one with another**, and the blood of Jesus Christ his Son cleanseth us from all sin" (I John 1:3-4 and 7).

The Poisoned Tulip
The Corporate/Vocational View of Election
Chapter Seven
Perseverance of the Saints

Many think that the Calvinist's doctrine of the perseverance of the saints is the same as the Bible doctrine of eternal security. The perseverance of the saints and the believer's eternal security are not the same doctrines although they propose the same outcomes. The *Westminster Confession of Faith* is the classic doctrinal statement of *Reformed Theology* and *Calvinism*.

"**I.** They, whom God has accepted in His Beloved, effectually called, and sanctified by His Spirit, can neither totally nor finally fall away from the state of grace, but shall certainly persevere therein to the end, and be eternally saved.

II. This perseverance of the saints **depends <u>not</u> upon their own free will, but upon the immutability of the decree of election**, flowing from the free and unchangeable love of God the Father; upon the efficacy of the merit and intercession of Jesus Christ, the abiding of the Spirit, and of the seed of God within them, and the nature of the covenant of grace: from all which arises also the certainty and infallibility thereof.

III. Nevertheless, they may, through the temptations of Satan and of the world, the **prevalency of corruption remaining in them, and the neglect of the means of their preservation**, fall into grievous sins; and, for a time, continue therein: whereby they incur God's displeasure, and grieve His Holy Spirit, come to be deprived of some measure of their graces and comforts, have their hearts hardened, and their consciences wounded; hurt and scandalize others, and bring temporal judgments upon themselves."[38] (Bolding added for emphasis.)

The Bible doctrine of eternal security is based upon what God gifts the believing sinner upon the instant of expressing the five verbs of saving faith: repent, believe, confess, call, and receive. To understand that the gift of eternal life is eternal, we must understand both the gifts of justification, which is God's righteousness *imparted* to the believer in the Person of the indwelling Spirit of Christ (II Peter 1:4) and *positional sanctification* before God "in Christ," the believer's High Priest. God promises that the indwelling Spirit of Christ will never leave (Hebrews 13:5, un-indwell) the "born again" believer. The indwelling Spirit of Christ is God's seal upon every believer until the day of the redemption of the body (Ephesians 4:30). This means the "born again" believer cannot be un-born again. Obviously, there is considerable difference between the Bible doctrine of eternal security and the Calvinist's doctrine of *perseverance of the saints* as stated in the *Westminster Confession of Faith*.

There is a constant and continual working of God's grace in the life of the "born again" believer known as God's preservation of that believer that is included in the gift of salvation. This preservation by God of the believer is promised in both the Old Testament books as well as in the New Testament.

"Thou *art* my hiding place; **thou shalt preserve me** from trouble; thou shalt compass me about with songs of deliverance. Selah" (Psalm 32:7).

---

[38] The *Westminster Confession of Faith* chapter seventeen in PDF downloaded from https://thewestminsterstandard.org/the-westminster-confession.

"[1] A Song of degrees. I will lift up mine eyes unto the hills, from whence cometh my help. [2] My help *cometh* from the LORD, which made heaven and earth. [3] He will not suffer thy foot to be moved: he that keepeth thee will not slumber. [4] Behold, he that keepeth Israel shall neither slumber nor sleep. [5] **The LORD *is* thy keeper:** the LORD *is* thy shade upon thy right hand. [6] The sun shall not smite thee by day, nor the moon by night. [7] **The LORD shall preserve thee from all evil: he shall preserve thy soul.** [8] **The LORD shall preserve thy going out and thy coming in from this time forth, and even for evermore**" (Psalm 121:1-8).

"[26] But ye believe not, because ye are not of my sheep, as I said unto you. [27] My sheep hear my voice, and I know them, and they follow me: [28] And **I give unto them eternal life; and they shall never perish, neither shall any *man* pluck them out of my hand.** [29] My Father, which gave *them* me, is greater than all; and **no *man* is able to pluck *them* out of my Father's hand.** [30] I and *my* Father are one" (John 10:26-30).

"[16] At my first answer no man stood with me, but all *men* forsook me: *I pray God* that it may not be laid to their charge. [17] Notwithstanding the Lord stood with me, and strengthened me; that by me the preaching might be fully known, and *that* all the Gentiles might hear: and I was delivered out of the mouth of the lion. [18] And the Lord shall deliver me from every evil work, and **will preserve *me* unto his heavenly kingdom**: to whom *be* glory for ever and ever. Amen" (II Timothy 4:16-18).

All these texts are common texts quoted to teach that the preservation of a believer's soul is unto eternal glorification and are valid texts to support the doctrine of eternal security. However, God's preservation of the "born again" believer's soul is not the same as the doctrine of eternal security, which is foundational to understanding what God gifts the believer when that believer is "born again." God gifts the believer a completed salvation POSITIONALLY. Nowhere is this truth made more evident than in Colossians 2:6-12.

"⁶ As ye have therefore received Christ Jesus the Lord, *so* walk ye in him: ⁷ Rooted and built up in him, and stablished in the faith, as ye have been taught, abounding therein with thanksgiving. ⁸ Beware lest any man spoil you through philosophy and vain deceit, after the tradition of men, after the rudiments of the world, and not after Christ. ⁹ For in him dwelleth all the fulness of the Godhead bodily. ¹⁰ And **ye are complete** {*perfect tense, passive voice, meaning a once for all forever act done by God*} **in him** {*the regeneration and baptism with the Spirit into the New Creation*}, which **is the head** {*new federal head of a new genesis*} of all principality and power: ¹¹ In whom also **ye are circumcised** {*aorist tense, passive voice, referring a Spirit accomplished event*} with the circumcision **made without hands**, in putting off the body of the sins of the flesh by the circumcision of Christ: ¹² **Buried with him in baptism** {*second aorist tense, passive voice, an event referring to baptism with the Spirit*} , wherein **also ye are risen** {*aorist tense, passive voice, a spiritual event*} with *him* through **the faith of the operation of God** {*God did these things explaining the passive voice in all these verbs*}, **who hath raised** {*aorist, active*} **him** {*Jesus*} from the dead" (Colossians 2:6-12).

The obvious intent of "complete" being in the perfect tense and passive voice in Colossians 2:10 is to communicate what is accomplished on behalf of the believer vicariously through "the regeneration" when each individual is "born again." Each of the three positionally accomplished realities are viewed by God as already accomplished in the lives of all "born again" believers. In other words, these positional realities are part of the gift of God in the gift of salvation and they are *once for all, forever,* or *eternal.* These positional realities are the foundation of the doctrine of the believer's eternal security "in Christ."

1. "circumcision made without hands"
2. "buried with him in baptism"
3. "risen with *him* through the faith of the operation of God"

The "born again" believer enters the New Covenant through the doorway of faith in the finish work of Jesus Christ. The believer is supernaturally "born again" into the New Covenant "through the faith of the operation of God." This new position is a "surety" (Hebrews 7:22) based upon the power of Jesus Christ and His position as the believer's representative High Priest after the eternal priestly order of Melchisedec. The point of Hebrews 7:11-28 is that the High Priesthood of Jesus before God is an **eternal representation** of what all "born again" believers are "in Christ." "By so much was Jesus made a surety of a better testament" (Hebrews 7:22). This "surety" is an eternal "surety" is based upon Christ's eternal position before God. Jesus' eternal position before God is the believer's eternal position before God. The word "surety" is God's guaranty of the believer's eternal security with the New Covenant "in Christ." **When the "born again" believer enters the New Covenant "in Christ" he/she enters an everlasting covenant secured by Jesus Christ.** This is the substance of the teaching in Hebrews chapters seven through Hebrews chapter ten.

"[S]urety--ensuring in His own person the certainty of the covenant to us. This He did by becoming responsible for our guilt, by sealing the covenant with His blood, and by being openly acknowledged as our triumphant Saviour by the Father, who raised Him from the dead. Thus He is at once God's surety for man, and man's surety for God, and so Mediator between God and man (Heb 8:6). **better**-- Heb 8:6; 13:20, 'everlasting.'"[39]

This is the fullest sense of the meaning of Christ's last proclamation on the Cross of Calvary; "it is finished {*tetelestai*}" (John 19:30). "It" is the fulfillment of the positional completeness of all the eternal, unconditional promises of God in the Abrahamic Covenant extending into the New Covenant, now positionally complete "in Christ."

"[11] If therefore perfection {*teleiôsis*} were by the Levitical priesthood, (for under it the people received the law,) what further need *was there* that another priest should rise after the order of Melchisedec, and not be called after the order of Aaron? [12] For the priesthood being changed, there is made of necessity a change also of the law. [13] For he of whom these things are spoken pertaineth to another tribe, of which no man gave attendance at the altar. [14] For *it is* evident that our Lord sprang out of Juda; of which tribe Moses spake nothing concerning priesthood. [15] And it is yet far more evident: **for that after the similitude of Melchisedec there ariseth another priest,** [16] **Who is made** {*second*

---

[39] Commentary Critical and Explanatory on the Whole Bible, Robert Jamieson, A.R. Fausset, and David Brown 1871, Abridged, single-volume edition, SwordSearcher\Modules\JFB.ss5cmty, Module file time: 8/2/2021 11:33:18 PM UTC.

perfect, active}, not after the law of a carnal commandment, but **after the power of an endless life**. [17] For he testifieth, Thou *art* a priest for ever after the order of Melchisedec. [18] For there is verily a disannulling of the commandment going before for the weakness and unprofitableness thereof. [19] For **the law made nothing perfect** {*finish or completed nothing*}, but the bringing in of **a better hope *did***; by the which we draw nigh unto God. [20] And inasmuch as not without an oath *he was made priest*: [21] (For **those** {*Levitical*} **priests were made without an oath** {*there was no promise from God that their priesthood was eternal*}; but this with an oath by him that said unto him, The Lord sware and will not repent, **Thou *art* a priest for ever after the order of Melchisedec**:) [22] **<u>By so much was Jesus made a surety of a better testament.</u>** [23] And they truly were many priests, because they were not suffered to continue by reason of death: [24] But this *man*, because **he continueth ever, hath an unchangeable priesthood**. [25] Wherefore **he is <u>able also to save them to the uttermost</u>** {*to the fullest extension*} **that come unto God by him, seeing he ever liveth to make intercession for them.** [26] For such an **high priest became us**, *who is* holy, harmless, undefiled, separate from sinners, and made higher than the heavens; [27] Who needeth not daily, as those high priests, to offer up sacrifice, first for his own sins, and then for the people's: **for this he did once** {*for all forever, see Hebrews 10:10, 12, 14, and 18*}, **when he offered up himself**. [28] For the law maketh men high priests which have infirmity; but the word of the oath, which was since the law, *maketh* the Son, **who is consecrated** {*perfect, passive*} **for evermore**" (Hebrews 7:11-28).

To understand the Bible doctrine of eternal security, we must understand what happens positionally to every genuine believer with a conversion of his/her heart the moment that person is "born again." This is why understanding the perfect tense and passive voice of salvation texts like Colossians 2:10 and "it is finished" {*tetelestai*} in John 19:30. Hebrews 7:11-28 is critical to understanding the doctrine of eternal security because the text presents the perfections given the believer in Jesus as our representative High Priest. In that context, we understand that sinners are not saved by their perfections, but by the perfections of Jesus who represents them before the Father. Therefore, because those believers have been baptized with/by the Spirit into Christ and the New Creation "in Christ," they have been baptized into His perfections.

"**¹⁴ For the love of Christ constraineth us** {*soon-ekh'-o, holds us together as believers compeling us to live for His purposes*}; because we thus judge, that if **one died for all, then were all dead**: ¹⁵ And *that* he died for all, that they which live should not henceforth live unto themselves, but unto him which died for them, and rose again. ¹⁶ **Wherefore henceforth know** {*perfect, active, meaning our perspective of others is radically changed from seeing people as merely good or bad and thereby judging their salvation according to false criteria*} **we no man after the flesh** {*in a purely empirical evaluation of anyone as to good or bad rather than by what they believe about Jesus and the Gospel*}: **yea, though we** {*some still living who had seen and heard Christ*} **have known Christ after the flesh** {*empirically*}, yet now **henceforth know we *him* no more** {*empirically, we cannot see Him or speak with Him in Person*}. ¹⁷ Therefore **if any man *be* in Christ** {*by grace through faith by being Spirit baptized into the*

New Creation 'in Christ'}, he is a **new creature** *{kainê ktisis, new of a different kind of a created thing}:* **old things are passed away** *{aorist, an event};* **behold** *{look, see, and understand the following statement for it is of great significance},* **all** **things are become** *{second perfect, active, meaning once for all forever <u>positionally</u> 'in Christ'}* **new** *{new of a different kind with different obligations, II Corinthians 5:14-15}.* [18] **And all things** *are* **of God** *{the believer's new position 'in Christ' are of God's doing by grace and they are already positionally 'finished' 'in Christ'},* who **hath reconciled** *{aorist, an event has happened}* us **to himself by Jesus Christ,** and **hath given to us** *{transition of responsibility from our High Priest to every believer-priest 'in Christ'}* **the ministry of reconciliation** *{see verse 15};* [19] **To wit** *{now defining the message of the 'ministry of reconciliation'},* that God was in Christ, reconciling the world unto himself, not imputing their trespasses unto them; and **hath committed unto us the word** *{logos; the message or the Gospel of Christ}* of reconciliation *{that once for all forever puts the believer into the New Creation}*" (II Corinthians 5:16-19).

The phrase "in Christ" as it is connected to the baptism with the Spirit is critical to understanding and confirming the eternal security of the genuinely ('if') "born again" believer. "<u>If</u> any man *be* in Christ" then "<u>all</u> things are become new" *{second perfect, active, meaning once for all forever <u>positionally</u> 'in Christ'}.* This is an operation of God that will not be reversed or canceled. It is already positionally "finished."

The event of salvation is defined by numerous actions accomplished by the Holy Spirit the moment a believing sinner repents, believes, confesses, calls, and

receives Christ. All these events are eternal gifts of salvation and none of these events are reversable because they are based upon the immutable promises of God. None of these events are based upon the perseverance or performance of the believer. Granted, the way a professing believer lives and what a professing believer believes may reveal he/she has never been truly "born again," but that does not mean anyone can reverse the miraculous work God does in the gift of salvation. Therefore, we must understand five terms or phrases used in the Bible that help us understand the "born again" believer's eternal security.

1. Regeneration

The word "regeneration" is found only two times in the New Testament books. First, in Matthew 19:28 used by Christ with the definite article "the regeneration." Second, it is used by Paul in Titus 3:5 where Paul describes a *bath* or *baptism* resulting from "regeneration." This *bath* or baptism does not generate or cause "regeneration." Regeneration generates/causes the *cleansing/washing*. **Clearly both texts and both uses of "regeneration" are referring to the baptism with/by the Holy Spirit that removes a condemned sinner from the first creation and immerses that person into the New Creation "in Christ."** When this spiritual immersion takes place, every aspect of the fall is positionally cleansed from the believer's life and that believer is positionally sanctified "in Christ" (Romans 5:1-2). **The baptism with the Spirit into "the regeneration" is what the phrase "born again" means. In other words, by the baptism with the Spirit the believer is supernaturally "born again" into "the regeneration."** Once this event of the *New Birth* has taken place, everything that has happened to our representative High Priest Jesus has ALREADY POSITIONALLY happened to the "born again" believer. This is the substance of the perfect tense and passive voice of "complete" in Colossians 2:10 and the phrase "<u>all</u> things are become new" in II Corinthians 5:17. Positionally, this is the full extension of the meaning of the perfect, passive of the phrase "it is finished" {*tetelestai*} in John 19:30. When God gives the believing sinner the gift of salvation, that gift must be viewed as a positionally finished gift that will never be rescinded and can never be changed. The "born again" believer cannot be un-born again. This is the doctrine of eternal security.

2. Spirit Baptism

The *baptism with the Holy Spirit* puts the believer into a *new existence* and a *new position* in the "body of Christ" (I Corinthians 12:13). This is not the same as the indwelling of the Holy Spirit. The *baptism with the Holy Spirit* is instantaneous and synchronous with a decision to trust in Christ. The *baptism with the Holy Spirit* provides the potential for all that is involved in the life of Jesus Christ.

It is not the baptism with the Holy Spirit that *empowers*. It is the "filling" that empowers. **The baptism with the Spirit merely places the believer in the *position* of power. The *position* provides the *potential*.** The gift of "eternal life" comes with the gift of eternal power. God's Spirit is the power in all that God does. When God's Word speaks of giving the believer "eternal life," God is speaking of the kind of life He possesses. "Eternal life" is the **perpetual God-life** given to the believer in the indwelling of the Spirit of God.

"[11] And **this is the record** {*evidence given of a surety*}, that God hath given to us **eternal life** {*perpetual or never ending life; life lived in perpetuity*}, and this life is **<u>in</u> his Son** {*by Spirit baptism into Christ and the New*

Creation of a new genealogy}. [12] **He that hath the Son**
{*indwelling Spirit of Christ*} **hath** {*perpetual*} **life**; *and*
he that hath not the Son of God hath not life" (I John
5:11-12).

**Although this eternal life "in Christ" is already in
our possession, the *power* of this eternal life lies in the
indwelling Holy Spirit of God. The *power* of this eternal
life is the Holy Spirit.** When the believer is "filled" with
Holy Spirit through practical sanctification by yielding his
will to God's will (Romans 6:11-13), the eternal life that is in
us in the Person of the Holy Spirit is released ("multiplied," II
Peter 1:2) through the believer's life. This releasing of *power*
(the eternal life of God or the *Christ-life*) is manifested
through the supernatural *enabling/empowering* of the yielded
believer. This dynamic is what Christ means by "let your light
so shine before men" (Matthew 5:16).

3. Justification

Justification is the gift of Christ's righteousness to the
believing sinner. Justification (Christ's gift of righteousness)
is received solely by grace and through the five verbs of faith;
repent, believe, confess, call, and receive Christ. The believer
is instantly indwelled by the Spirit of Christ imparting to that
believer the righteousness of Jesus Christ in the Person of the
Holy Spirit. Again, the gift of the indwelling Spirit of God as
the righteousness of Jesus Christ in justification is a *once for
all forever gift*. This is shown to us in II Peter 1:3-4 by the
use by the perfect tense and passive voice on two occasions.
The perfect tense shows us God's gift is non-rescindable.

"[1] Simon Peter, a servant and an apostle of Jesus Christ,
to them that have obtained like precious faith with us
through the righteousness of God and our Saviour Jesus

Christis: [2] **Grace and peace be multiplied** unto you **through the knowledge** {*experiential relational*} of God, and of Jesus our Lord, [3] According **as his divine power hath given** {*perfect, passive; once for all forever*} unto us all things that *pertain* unto life and godliness, through the knowledge of him that hath called us to glory and virtue: [4] Whereby **are given** {*perfect, passive; once for all forever*} unto us exceeding great and precious promises: **that by these ye might be partakers of the divine nature**, having escaped the corruption that is in the world through lust" (II Peter 1:1-4).

4. Sealed with the Spirit

The indwelling Holy Spirit of God is the believer's eternal possession of Christ and God's promise of eternal security "in Christ." In that indwelling, God has created the most intimate relationship that can ever possibly be experienced. God promises that he "will never leave nor forsake" this intimate relationship. **This relationship is eternal.** In fact, God compares it to a marriage relationship in Hebrews 13:4-6 and gives a warning about unfaithfulness in the beginning of the text.

The point of Hebrews 13:4-6 in both its promise and warning is that the believer's union connects intimately to both the omnipresence and omniscience of God in the believer's life actions. The promise is that no matter what the believer does, God will not "leave thee, nor forsake thee." The warning is, because of the intimate union with God, He will also know every sinful thought, motivation, and act and will "judge" accordingly with appropriate chastisement. Examples of such instances are Lot, David, Solomon, and Samson, etc.

"⁴ Marriage *is* honourable in all, and the bed undefiled: but whoremongers and adulterers God will judge. ⁵ *Let your* conversation *be* without covetousness; *and be* content with such things as ye have: for he hath said, **I will never leave thee, nor forsake thee.** ⁶ So that we may boldly say, **The Lord *is* my helper** {*God is there to help or aid in any way He deems necessary*}, and I will not fear what man shall do unto me" (Hebrews 13:4-6).

"²⁰ For all **the promises of God** in him *are* **yea** {*yes*}, and **<u>in him</u> Amen** {*let it be so*}, unto the glory of God **by us**. ²¹ Now **he which stablisheth** {*present, active; is stabilizing in our union with Christ*} us with you **in Christ** {*the New Creation*}, and hath anointed us {*aorist, active; positionally consecrated believers for service as believer-priests*}, *is* God; ²² Who **hath <u>also</u>** {*plus the other promises already listed*} **sealed** {*aorist, an event for security or preservation purposes*} us, **and given** {*aorist, an event of another plus*} **the** {*not 'a'*} **earnest** {*a security deposit to ensure future fulfillment of all promises*} of **the Spirit <u>in</u>** our **hearts** {*referring to the indwelling Spirit of Christ*}" (II Corinthians 1:20-22).

The grand failure of the teaching of the false doctrine of the *perseverance of the saints* is that it fails to teach eternal security according to the "finished" gift God gives when He gives salvation to the sinner. Therefore, no Calvinist can ever be sure that he is one of God's elect until he perseveres to the end (death). Although he believes his salvation is totally dependent upon God's choice, he can never truly know he is one of the chosen ones until he finally stands before God. *Perseverance of the saints* is neither the doctrine of eternal security nor assurance of salvation (I John 3:19).

"[3] Blessed *be* the God and Father of our Lord Jesus Christ, **who hath blessed us** {*aorist, active; an event*} with **all spiritual blessings in heavenly** *places* **in Christ:** [4] According as **he hath chosen us in him** {*as priests vocationally*} before the foundation of the world, that we should be holy and without blame before him in love: [5] Having **predestinated us unto the adoption of children** {*placement as mature believers to minister as believer-priests*} by Jesus Christ to himself, according to the good pleasure of his will, [6] To the praise of the glory of his grace, wherein **he hath made us accepted** {*positional sanctification*} **in the beloved** {*Christ as our representative High Priest in Heaven*}. [7] **In whom** {*Christ as our High Priest in Heaven*} **we have** {*present tense*} redemption through his blood, **the forgiveness of sins** {*aphesis, word used for remission of the penalty of sins in salvation, not the forgiveness of sins in restoration to fellowship*}, according to the riches of his grace; [8] Wherein **he hath abounded** {*aorist, context is in salvation*} toward us in all wisdom and prudence; [9] **Having made known** {*aorist, context is in salvation*} **unto us the mystery of his will** {*the 'mystery' here now revealed and explained is the priesthood of all Church Age believer 'in Christ'*}, according to his good pleasure which he hath purposed in himself: [10] **That in the dispensation of the fulness of times** {*the end of this creation and the beginning of the New Creation after the Millennial Kingdom*} he might gather together **in one all things in Christ**, both which are in heaven, and which are on earth; *even* in him: [11] In whom also we have obtained an inheritance, **being predestinated** {*to glorification*} according to the purpose of him who worketh all things after the counsel of his own will: [12] That **we should be to the praise of his glory** {*as the primary ministry as believer-priests*}, **who first trusted** {*the 'church of the firstborn', Hebrews 12:23*} in Christ. [13] In whom ye also *trusted*, after that ye heard the word of truth, the gospel of your salvation: in whom also **after that ye believed, ye were sealed with** {*the indwelling*} **that holy Spirit of promise,** [14] Which {*Holy Spirit*} is **the earnest** {*surety, or God's signature of promise*} of our inheritance until **the redemption of the purchased possession** {*glorification of the body, Romans 8:23 and I Corinthians 6:19*}, unto the praise of his glory" (Ephesians 1:3-14).

5. Positionally Sanctified "in Christ"

One of the greatest misnomers and false doctrines is the teaching that the security of a believer's salvation somehow rests in his continual practical sanctification before God. There are enumerable *sects* (denominations) of professed Christianity that teach variations of this false doctrine.

Understanding the transition from the doctrine of justification in Romans chapters three and four into the doctrine of perfect and positional sanctification in Romans chapter five is critically important to understanding the eternality of the justified believer's new *standing* (Romans 5:2) in Christ.

There is a reason why we must understand the transition from justification by grace through faith into *perfect positional* **and** *eternal sanctification* **by grace through faith in the impartation of the righteousness of Jesus Christ through the indwelling Spirit of Christ. The reason is because the believer's eternal security is based upon his positional sanctification in Christ.** The believer's eternal security is not based upon his practical sanctification. If the believer's eternal security was based upon practical sanctification, the believer would lose his salvation every time that sanctification was defiled. In such a case, the believer would need to be "born again" again. What a fiasco of the gift of salvation this falsehood would create.

"[1] Therefore **being** {*standing*} **justified** {aorist, passive} by faith, we have peace with God **through our Lord Jesus Christ:** [2] By whom also **we have** {*perfect, active; cannot change*} access by faith **into this grace wherein we stand** {*perfect, active; cannot change*}, and **rejoice in hope** of the glory of God {*redemption of the body and glorification*} [3] **And not only** *so,* **but we glory in tribulations also**: knowing that tribulation worketh patience; [4] And patience, experience; and experience, hope: [5] And hope maketh not ashamed; because the love of God is shed abroad in our hearts by the Holy Ghost **which is given** {*aorist, passive*} unto us" (Romans 5:1-5).

Romans chapter five begins to make the transition from the practical new standing "in grace" because of the gift of justification to the doctrine of spiritual growth. **The doctrine of spiritual growth is called the doctrine of sanctification. We do not grow in our perfect sanctification gifted to us in justification because positional sanctification is already perfect. We grow in our practical sanctification as we learn to live what we learn through the enabling of the indwelling Spirit of Christ.**

Why is understanding that justification, which is the gift of the perfect righteousness of Jesus Christ to the believing sinner, is also perfect positional sanctification before God "in Christ Jesus" in the New Birth? Why is knowing this a critical truth? It is important because both justification and positional perfect sanctification result from a **SINGLE WORK** of grace in salvation. Yes, God's enabling grace continues through the working of His indwelling Spirit to enable the yielded believer (Romans 6:11-13) to have victory over his/her sin nature, but **this is all just an extension of the single work of grace in the believer's regeneration.** There is no second work of grace or third work of grace (*ad infinium*) as some teach today.

Bibliography

Airola, Paavo, *Are You Confused?,* Health Plus, Publishers, Twenty-First Printing, September 1995.

Alford, Henry, *Alford's Greek Testament, Hebrews-Revelation,* Volume I, Volume II, Volume III, Volume IV, Baker Book House; reprinted 1980.

American Baptist Quarterly, *A Confession of Faith,* American Baptist Historical Society, Copyright 2002.

Archer, Gleason L., *Encyclopedia of Bible Difficulties.* The Zondervan Corporation Copyright 1982.

Armitage, Thomas, *The History of the Baptists, Volume I, Volume II,* Maranatha Baptist Press, Reprint 1980.

Armstrong, John H. -General Editor, *The Coming Evangelical Crisis,* Moody Bible Institute, Copyright 1996.

Armstrong, Mead C., *That Ye Might Walk Worthy-Studies in Colossians,* Regular Baptist Press, Copyright 1981.

Armstrong, O.K. and Marjorie M. Armstong, *The Indomitable Baptists,* Doubleday & Company, Inc., Copyright 1967.

Augustine, *The Confessions of Saint Augustine,* The Christian Library, 1984.

Baker, Don, *Finding Hope In Times of Crisis,* Inspirational Press, Copyright 1992.

Barclay, William, *The Letters to Timothy, Titus, and Philemon, revised edition-The Daily Study Series,* The Westminster Press, Copyright 1975.

Barclay, William, *The Letters of James and Peter, revised edition-The Daily Study Series,* The Westminster Press, Copyright 1975.

Barber, Cyril J., *Everyman's Bible Commentary-Habakkuk and Zephaniah,* Moody press, Copyright 1985.

Barnes, Albert, *Genesis; Barnes' Notes on the Old & New Testament,* Vol. 1, Baker Book House, twentieth printing 1980.

Genesis; Barnes' Notes on the Old & New Testament, Vol. 2, Baker Book House, eighteenth printing 1980.

Exodus-Ruth; Barnes' Notes on the Old & New Testament, Vol. 1, Baker Book House, eighteenth printing 1980.

Samuel-Esther; Barnes' Notes on the Old & New Testament, Vol. 1, Baker Book House, seventeenth printing 1980.

Job; Barnes' Notes on the Old & New Testament, Vol. 1, Baker Book House, seventeenth printing 1980.

Job; Barnes' Notes on the Old & New Testament, Vol. 2, Baker Book House, sixteenth printing 1980.

Psalms; Barnes' Notes on the Old & New Testament, Vol. 1, Baker Book House, seventeenth printing 1980.

Psalms; Barnes' Notes on the Old & New Testament, Vol. 2, Baker Book House, sixteenth printing 1980.

Psalms; Barnes' Notes on the Old & New Testament, Vol. 3, Baker Book House, sixteenth printing 1980.

Proverbs-Ezekiel; Barnes' Notes on the Old & New Testament, Vol. 1, Baker Book House, sixteenth printing 1980.

Isaiah; Barnes' Notes on the Old & New Testament, Vol. 1, Baker Book House, sixteenth printing 1980.

Isaiah; Barnes' Notes on the Old & New Testament, Vol. 2, Baker Book House, seventeenth printing 1980.

Daniel; Barnes' Notes on the Old & New Testament, Vol. 1, Baker Book House, sixteenth printing 1980.

Daniel; Barnes' Notes on the Old & New Testament, Vol. 2, Baker Book House, fifteenth printing 1980.

Minor Prophets; Barnes' Notes on the Old & New Testament, Vol. 1, Baker Book House, seventeenth printing 1980.

Minor Prophets; Barnes' Notes on the Old & New Testament, Vol. 2, Baker Book House, eighteenth printing 1980.

Matthew-Mark; Barnes' Notes on the Old & New Testament, Vol. 1, Baker Book House, fourth printing 1981.

Luke-John; Barnes' Notes on the Old & New Testament, Vol. 1, Baker Book House, twenty-third printing 1980.

Acts; Barnes' Notes on the Old & New Testament, Vol. 1, Baker Book House, eighteenth printing 1980.

Romans; Barnes' Notes on the Old & New Testament, Vol. 1, Baker Book House, seventeenth printing 1980.

1 Corinthians; Barnes' Notes on the Old & New Testament, Vol. 1, Baker Book House, seventeenth printing 1980.

11 Corinthians and Galatians; Barnes' Notes on the Old & New Testament, Vol. 1, Baker Book House, sixteenth printing 1980.
Ephesians-Colossians; Barnes' Notes on the Old & New Testament, Vol. 1, Baker Book House, seventeenth printing 1980.
Hebrews; Barnes' Notes on the Old & New Testament, Vol. 1, Baker Book House, seventeenth printing 1980.
Thessalonians-Philemon; Barnes' Notes on the Old & New Testament, Vol. 1, Baker Book House, sixteenth printing 1980.
James-Jude; Barnes' Notes on the Old & New Testament, Vol. 1, Baker Book House, twentieth printing 1981.
Revelation; Barnes' Notes on the New Testament, Vol. 1, Baker Book House, twentieth printing 1981.

Barnhart, Clarence L.-Editor, *Thorndike Barnhart Comprehensive Desk Dictionary,* Scott, Foresman and Company, Copyright 1955.

Barnhouse, Donald Grey, *God's Methods for Holy Living,* Revelation Publications, Copyright 1940.

Baumgartner, Anne S., *A Comprehensive Dictionary of the Gods,* Wings Books, 1995 Edition.

Baxter, Sidlow J., *Explore the Book-Six Volumes in One,* Zondervan Publishing House Eleventh Printing March 1975.

Beacham, Roy E. and Bauder, Kevin T., *One Bible Only?,* William B Eerdmans Publishing Company Copyright 1962.

Beasley-Murray, G.R., *Baptism in the New Testament,* Jerry W. Beaver Printed 2009.

Bednar, L., *Evidence of the Divine Hand on True Scripture,* Lawrence Bednar, Copyright 2010.

Binney, Jim, *Living Purely in an Impure World,* The Counselor's Pen Publications, Copyright 2003.

Boer, Harry R., *A Short History of the Early Church,* Wm. B. Eerdmans Pub. Co., 5th Printing, April 1981.

Boettner, Loraine, *The Millennium,* Presbyterian and Reformed Publishing Company, Revised Addition 1984.

Boice, James Montgomery, *An Expositional Commentary-Philippians,* Zondervan Publishing House, Copyright 1971.
The Minor Prophets-Volume 2-Mich-Malachi, Zondervan Publishing House, Copyright 1986.

Bopp, Virgil W., *Confidently Committed-A Look at the Baptist Heritage,* Regular Baptist Press, Copyright 1987.

Borland, James A., *Christ In The Old Testament,* Moody Press, Copyright 1978.

Bounds, E.M., *E.M. Bounds on Prayer,* Whitaker House, Copyright 1997.

Brandenburg, Kent-Editor, *Thou Shalt Keep Them-A Biblical Theology of the Perfect Preservation of Scripture,* Pillar & Ground Publishing, Published 2003.

Breeze, Dave, *Seven Men Who Rule the World from the Grave,* Moody Press, 8th Printing, 1995.
Satan's Ten Most Believable Lies, Moody Press, Paperback edition 1987.

Bruce, F.F., *Jesus: Lord and Savior,* Intervarsity Press, 1966.
The Hard Sayings of Jesus, Intervarsity Press, 1983.

Bruns, Roger A., *Preacher-Billy Sunday & Big-Time American Evangelism,* W.W. Norton & Company, Copyright 1992.

Bruce, A.B, *The Training of the Twelve,* Kregel Publications, Seventh Printing 1978.

Bruce, F.F., *The Epistles of John,* F.F. Bruce, 1970.
Bruce, F.F., *What The Bible Teaches About What Jesus Did,* Tyndale House Publishers, 1979.
Bruce, F.F., *Paul Apostle of the Heart Set Free,* William B. Eerdmans Publishing Company, Reprinted 1983.
Bruce, F.F., *The Canon of Scripture,* 1988.

Brumback, Carl, *What Meaneth This?,* Gospel Publishing House, Copyright 1947.

Bucke, Emory Stevens-Editor, *The Interpreter's Dictionary of the Bible,* Abingdon, Copyright 1976.

Burgon, Dean John William, *Inspiration and Interpretation,* The Dean Burgon Society Press, Copyright 1999.
The Traitional Text of the Holy Gospels-Volume I, The Dean Burgon Society Press, Copyright 1998.

Burnham, David and Sue Burnham, *Acts the Body in Action-A Group Bible Study,* Moody Press, Copyright 1978.

Dean Burgon, *The Last Twelve Verses of Mark,* James Parker and Co., Copyright 1871 Reprinted.

Dean Burgon, *The Causes of Corruption of the Traditional Test of the Holy Gospels-Volume II,* The Dean Burgon Society Press, Copyright 1998.

Carson, D.A., *The King James Version Debate A Plea for Realism,* Baker Book House, Thirteenth Printing 1995.
Exegetical Fallacies Second Edition, Baker Book House, Seventh Printing 2002.

Central Baptist Theological Seminary-Faculty, *The Bible Version Debate-The Perspective of Central Baptist Theological Seminary,* Copyright 1997.

Chafer, Lewis Sperry, *Systematic Theology, Volume I, Volume II, Volume III, Volume IV, Volume V, Volume VI, Volume VII, Volume VIII,* Lewis Sperry Chafer, Thirteenth Printing 1976.
Salvation, Lewis Sperry Chafer, Copyright 1917.

Charnock, Stephen, *Existence and Attributes of God-Volume I,* Baker Book House, Reprinted 1979.
Existence And Attributes of God-Volume II, Baker Book House, Third Printing May 1981.

Chilstrom, Herbert W., *Hebrews- A New & Better Way,* Fortress Press, Copyright 1984.

Christian, John T., *A History of the Baptists, Volume I,* Bogard Press, Copyright 1922.
Volume II, Bogard Press, Copyright 1926.

Clearwaters, Richard V., *The Local Church of the New Testament,* Central Press, Copyright 1954.
The Great Conservative Baptist Compromise, Central Seminary Press.
On The Upward Road- An Autobiography, Nystrom Publishing, 1954.

Cloud, David W., *Myths about the Modern Bible Versions,* Published by Way of Life Literature, Copyright 1999 Second Edition Sept.1999.

Cocoris, Michael G., *Evangelism: A Biblical Approach,* Moody Press, 1984.

Coder, Maxwell S., *Jude-The Acts of the Apostates,* Moody Press, Copyright 1958.

Cohen, Gary G. and Salem Kirban, *Revelation Visualized,* Salem Kirban, Copyright 1981.

Coleman, Robert E.-Editor, *Evangelism on the Cutting Edge,* Fleming H. Revell Company, Copyright 1986.

Comfort, Philip W., *Early Manuscripts & Modern Translations of the New Testament,* Tyndale House Publishers, Inc. Copyright 1990.

Comfort, Ron, *Last Things A Book on Bible Prophecy,* Ron Comfort Evangelistic Association, 2011.
Revival's Golden Key, Bridge-Logos Pub, 2002.

Conybeare, W.J. and Howson J.S., *The Life and Epistles of St. Paul,* WM. B. Eerdmans Publishing Company, Reprinted December 1992.

Cook, Arnold L., *Historical Drift Must My Church Die?,* Christian Publications, 2000.

Corner, Daniel D., *The Believer's Conditional Security,* Evangelical Outreach, Copyright 2000.

Couch, Mal, *Dictionary of Premillennial Theology,* Kregel, 1996.
A Bible Handbook to The Acts of The Apostles, Kregel, 1999.
An Introduction to Classical Evangelical Hermeneutics, Kregel, 2000.

Cowman, Charles E., *Handfuls of Purpose,* Cowman Publications, Copyright 1955.

Cowen, Gerald, *Salvation-Word Studies From The Greek New Testament,* Broadman Press, Copyright 1990.

Criswell, W.A., *Isaiah and exposition,* Zondervan Publishing House, 1982.
The Bible for Today's World, Zondervan Publishing House, Third printing, 1966.
Why I Preach That the Bible Is Literally True, Broadman Press, Copyright 1969.

Crockett, William Day, *A Harmony of Samuel, Kings and Chronicles,* Baker Book House, Fourteenth Printing, 1978.

Crow, Paul, *Cliffs and Fences-Holiness and Personal Separation In Biblical Perspective,* Booksurge, Copyright 2008.

Dabney, Robert L., *Lectures In Systematic Theology,* Zondervan Publishing House, Third printing, 1976.

Davis, John J., *Moses and the Gods of Egypt-Studies in Exodus-second edition,* Baker Books, Copyright 1971.

DeHaan, M.R., *Coming Events in Prophecy,* Zondervan Publishing House, Tenth printing, November 1970.
Hebrews-Twenty-six Simple Studies in God's Pattern for Victorious Living, Zondervan Publishing House, Copyright 1959.

Delany, James, *Abiding in Christ-God's Plan for Spiritual Growth,* James Delany, Copyright 2000.

DeJong, Benjamin R., Director of Material, *This We Believe,* IFCA Publications, Revised 1980.

DeMar, Gary and Peter Leithart, *The Reduction of Christianity,* Dominion Press, Copyright 1988.

Dersham, James-Managing Editor, *So Great Salvation,* Regular Baptist Press, 1986.

Dollar, George W., *The New Testament and New Pentecostalism,* Central Baptist Theological Seminary, Copyright 1978.

Dowley, Tim- Organizing Editor, *Eerdmans Handbook to the History of Christianity,* William B. Publishing Co., Reprinted 1987.

Dunn, Richard S., *The Age of Religious Wars, 1559-1689,* Norton & Company, Inc., Copyright 1970.

Eaide, John, *Thessalonians,* James and Klock Christian Publishing Co., Reprint 1977.
Philippians, James and Klock Christian Publishing Co., Reprint 1977.
Galatians, James and Klock Christian Publishing Co., Reprint 1977.

Earle, Ralph, *Word Meanings in the New Testament- Volume 1, Matthew, Volume 2 Mark, Luke, Volume 3 Romans, Volume 4, 1, and 2 Corinthians, Galatians, Ephesians, Volume 5, Philippians, Colossians, 1 & 2 Thessalonians, Volume 6, 1 & 2 Timothy, Titus, Philemon,* Baker Book House Company, Reprinted 1980.

Clarke, Adam, *Adam Clarke's Commentary on the Bible,* Baker Book House Company, Fifteenth Printing 1984.

Edersheim, Alfred, *Old Testament Bible History,* William B. Eerdmans Publishing Company, Reprinted December 1982.
Practical Truths from Elisha, Kregel Publications, Copyright 1982.

Epp, Theodore H., *Volume 1 Practical Studies in Revelation,* Back to the Bible, Copyright 1969.
Present Labor and Future Reward, Back to the Bible, Copyright 1960.
Joshua Victorious by Faith, Back to the Bible, Copyright 1968.
Joseph -God planned it for good, The Good News Broadcasting Association, Copyright 1971.

Epp, Eldon Jay and Gordon D. Fee-Edited by, *New Testament Textual Criticism,* Clarendon Press, 1981.

Evans, William, *Personal Soul Winning-A Guide To Effective Methods,* Moody Press, Revised 1964.

Farison, Marquerite, *Passport To Heaven,* Barbour Books, Copyright 1989.

Farrar, Canon, *The Story of A Beautiful Life,* Dodd, Mead and Company, Copyright 1900.

Farrar, Steve, *Finishing Strong,* Dodd, Mead and Company, Copyright 1995.

Farrar, F.W., *Texts Explained or Helps to Understand the New Testament,* Dodd, Mead and Company, Copyright 1899.

Farrell, Tom, *Preaching That Pleases God The Keys to Life-Changing Bible Exposition,* Striving Together Publications, Copyright 2010.

Finney, Charles G., *Revivals,* Fleming H. Revell Company, 1965.

Fosdick, Harry Emerson, *Christianity and Progress,* Fleming H. Revell Company, Copyright 1922.

Fraser, John W. -Translator
Calvin's New Testament Commentaries-Volume 6-Acts 1-13
Calvin's New Testament Commentaries-Volume 7-Acts 14-28
Calvin's New Testament Commentaries-Volume 9- I Corinthians
Calvin's New Testament Commentaries-Volume 11-Galatians, Ephesians, Philippians, & Colossians
Calvin's New Testament Commentaries-Volume 12-Hebrews and 1 & 2 Peter, William B, Eerdmans Publishing Company, 1965.

Gaebelein, Frank E.- General Editor, *The Expositor's Bible Commentary, Ephesians-Philemon, Volume II – NIV,* Zondervan Publishing House, 1978.
Volume 7 with NIV - The Expositor's Bible Commentary, Zondervan Publishing House, 1985.

Gardiner, Gardiner E., *The Corinthian Catastrophe,* Kregel Publications, 1974.

Garlock, Frank and Woetzel Kurl, *Music in the Balance,* Majesty Music, Inc., Second Printing 1996.

Garraty, John A. and Gay, Peter (Editors), *The Columbia History of the World,* Harper and Row Publishers, 1987.

Gaussen, L., *Divine Inspiration of the Bible,* Kregel, Copyright 1971.

Garrison, R. Benjamin, *Creeds In Collision,* Abington Books, 1967.

Gentry, Kenneth L. Jr., *The Greatness of the Great Commission,* Kenneth L. Gentry, Revised edition 1993.

Getz, Gene A., *The Measure of a Church,* G.L. Regal Books, 7th Printing, 1979.
Sharpening the focus of the Church, Moody Press, 1974.

Gibbs, Alfred P., *The Preacher and His Preaching,* Walterick Publishers, 6th Edition.

Gillquist, Peter E., *Love Is Now,* Zondervan Publishing House, Third Printing 1971.

Gilmore, John, *The Probing Heaven-Key Questions on the Hereafter,* Baker Book House, Copyright 1989.

Goetsch, John, *Twenty-first Century Revival (is it possible?),* West Coast Baptist College.

Good, Kenneth H., *God's Blueprint for a Church-A Study of Baptist Distinctives,* Regular Baptist Press.

Grady, William P., *Final Authority-A Christian's Guide to the King James Bible,* Grady Publications, Eighth Printing 1997.

Grant, George, *In The Shadow of Plenty,* Christian Liberty Press, Revised Edition 1998.

Green, Michael, *Evangelism in the Early Church,* Wm. B. Eerdmans Pub. Co., Reprinted Jan. 1985.

Greenhough, M.A., Thomas G. Selby, Albert Goodrich, Alexander Stewart, George Milligan, W.H. Selbie, J. Morgan Gibbon, Alfred Rowland, D Rowlands, *The Sermon on the Mount A Practical Exposition of St. Matthew VI 16-VII 27,* Manchester James Robinson, 1903.

Grist, William Alexander, *The Historic Christ in The Faith of To-day,* Fleming H. Revell Company, Copyright 1911.

Griswold, Roland, E., *The Winning Church,* Victor Books, Copyright 1986.

Gundry, Stanley N. and Alan F. Johnson-Editors, *Tensions In Contemporary Theology,* Moody Press, Copyright 1976.

Habershon, Ada R., *The Study of The Miracles,* Kregel, Fourth Printing 1972.

Haifley, Daniel S., *The Bible Study Toolbook-A Text on Biblical Hermeneutics,* Beams of Grace Press, Fourth Printing 2009.

Halfyard, Samuel F., *Fundamentals of the Christian Religion,* Jennings and Graham, Copyright 1911.

Hartog, John, *The Fall of a Kingdom-Jeremiah and Lamentations,* Regular Baptist Press, 1983.

Hendricks, Howard G., *Don't Fake It: Say It With Love the art and joy of Telling the Good News,* Victor Books, Third Printing 1973.

Hengstenberg, E.W., *Christology of The Old Testament,* Kregel Publications, Third Printing, 1976.

Henry, Carl F.G., *Fundamentals of the Faith,* Baker Book House 1975.

Hester, H.L., *The Heart of the New Testament,* Loizeaux Brothers, Third Edition, 1980.

Hislop, Alexander, *The Two Babylons,* Loizeaux Brothers, Third Edition, 1989.

Hoekstra, Harvey T., *The World Council of Churches and the Demise of Evangelism,* Tyndale House, Copyright 1979.

Holstad, Wayne B., *Leviticus v. Leviathan-Choosing Our Sovereign* Alethos Press, Copyright 2004.

Horne, Chevis F., *Crisis in the Pulpit,* Baker Book House, Copyright 1975.

Huffman, J.A., *Redemption Completed,* The Standard Press, Eighth Edition, 1941.
Wholly Living-Paul's Last Word for a Dynamic Lifestyle, Victor Books, 1978.

Hufhand, Lawrence D., *The Acts of the Apostates-A Study in the book of Jude,* Lift Ministries, 2011.

Hunt, Dave and McMahon, T.A., *The Seduction of Christianity,* Harvest House Publishers, 6th Printing, Feb. 1986.

Hunnex, Milton D., *Existentialism and Christian Belief-A Frank Appraisal of a Modern-Day Philosophy,* Moody Press, 1969.

Hunter, Harold F., *Revelation,* Trinty Crusades for Christ, 1984.

Hunter, John E., *Living the Christ filled Life,* Zondervan Publishing House, Tenth Printing 1975.
Ironside, H.A., *Lectures on Levitical Offerings,* Loizeaux Brothers, Tenth Printing 1979.
Holiness-The False and the True, Loizeaux Brothers, Twenty-third Printing 1980.

Jackson, Bill, *Battling for Eternity-The Church's Quest for Pure Evangelism,* Colonial Baptist Press, Copyright 1992.
Scriptural Evangelism, Colonial Baptist Press, Copyright 1992.

Jackson, Jeremy C., *No Other Foundation, The Church Through Twenty Centuries,* Cornerstone Books, 1980.

Jackson, Paul R., *The Doctrine and Administration of the Church,* Regular Baptist Press, Sixth Printing, 1997.

Jacobs, Jack W., *What's Right with the Church-Studies in Ephesians,* Regular Baptist Press, Copyright, 1980.

James, Edgar C., *Day of the Lamb,* Victor Books, Third Printing, 1981.

James, Kevin R., *The Corruption of the Word: The Failure of Modern New Testament Scholarship,* Micro-Load Press, Third Printing, 1995.

Jank, Margaret, *Culture Shock,* Moody Press, Copyright 1977.

Jefferson, Charles, *The Minister As Shepherd,* Scripture Truth Book Co., 2006.

Jensen, Irving L., *Romans-A Self-Study Guide,* Moody Bible Institute, Copyright 1969.

Jenson, Ron and Jim Stevens, *Dynamics of Church Growth,* Baker Book House, Copyright 1981.

Jewish Nation, *Hebrew English New Covenant-Prophecy Edition,* Hope of Israel Publications, 2003.

Johnson, Cedric B. and H. Newton Malony, *Christian Conversion: Biblical and Psychological Perspectives,* Zondervan Publishing House, Copyright 1982.

Johnson, Daniel R., *The Greatest Soldier Who Ever Lived,* Providence Publications, Fourth Printing 2001.

Juris, Paul, *Blessed Mary,* Paul Juris, Copyright 1978.
The Other Side of Purgatory, Paul Juris, Copyright 1981.

Kaiser, Walter C. Jr., *Malachi God's Unchanging Love,* Baker Book House, Copyright 1984.

Keddie, Gordon, *Looking for The Good Life-The Search for Fulfillment in the Light of Ecclesiastes,* Presbyterian and Reformed Publishing Company, Copyright 1991.

Keller, Phillip W., *A Layman Looks at the Lord's Prayer,* World Wide Publications, Third Printing, Second Printing 1976.

Kent, Homer A. Jr., *The Pastoral Epistles-Studies in 1 Timothy and 2 Timothy and Titus,* BMH Books, Copyright 1995.

Kidner, Derek, *An Introduction To Wisdom Literature-The Wisdom of Proverbs, Job & Ecclesiastes,* IVP, Copyright 1985.

Kinder, Ernst, *Evangelical-What Does It Really Mean,* Concordia Publishing House, Copyright 1968.

King, Richard and Susan, *Confusion-A Biblical Critique of the New Teaching of Dr. Peter Ruckman,* Gigatt Books, Copyright 2012.

Kistemaker, Simon J., *New Testament Commentary Acts,* Baker Book House, Copyright 1990.

Kittel, Gerhard-Editor, *Volume I-Theological Dictionary of the New Testament,* WM. B. Eerdmans Publishing Company, Reprinted September 1983.

Klimkeit, Hans-Joachim, *Gnosis on the Silk Road,* Hans J. Klimkeit, Copyright 1993.

Knauss, Keith E., *Heartbeats of the Holy-A Philosophy Of Ministry,* Dickerson Press Inc., 2009.

Kuen, Alfred F., *I Will Build My Church,* Moody Press, Translated from original French Edition, 1971.

Kuhne, Gary W., *The Dynamics of Discipleship Training-Being and Producing Spiritual Leaders,* Zondervan Publishing House, Copyright 1978 (two copies).

LaHaye, Tim, *Revelation,* Zondervan Publishing House, tenth printing, 1978.
The Battle for the Family, Fleming H. Revell Company, 1984.

Lawson, George, *Exposition of Proverbs,* Kregel Inc., Printed 1980.

Lewis, C.S., *Mere Christianity,* Macmillan Publishing Co. Inc., 1986.

Lightfoot, J. B. and Harmer, J.R. (Translator), *The Apostolic Fathers (Second Edition),* Baker Book House Co., Second Printing, Aug. 1990.

Lightfoot, Neil R., *How We Got the Bible (Second Edition),* Baker Book House Co., Third Printing, Dec. 1991.

Lindsey, Hal, *The Late Great Planet Earth,* Zondervan Publishing House, 27th Printing, Feb. 1974.
The Terminal Generation, Fleming H. Revell Company, Copyright 1976.

Lloyd-Jones, Martyn D., *Life in the Spirit in Marriage, Home & Work,* Baker Book House, Reprinted 1975.
The Christian Soldier-An Exposition of Ephesians 6:10-20, Baker Book House, Reprinted 1978.

God's Ultimate Purpose-An Exposition of Ephesians One, Baker Book House, Reprinted 1979.
The Unsearchable Riches of Christ-An Exposition of Ephesians 3:1-21, Baker Book House, Reprinted 1980.
Christian Unity-An Exposition of Ephesians 4:1-16, Baker Book House, Reprinted 1981.
Romans-Atonement and Justification-Exposition of Chapters 3:20-4:25, Zondervan Publishing House, Ninth Printing, 1981.
Romans-Assurance-Exposition of Chapter 5, Zondervan Publishing House, Ninth Printing, 1980.
Romans-The New Man-Exposition of Chapter 6, Zondervan Publishing House, Ninth Printing, 1981.
Romans-The Law: It's Functions and Limits-Exposition of Chapters 7:1-8:4, Zondervan Publishing House, Ninth Printing, 1981.
Romans-The Sons of God-Exposition of Chapters 8:5-17, Zondervan Publishing House, Seventh Printing, 1981.
Romans-The Final Perseverance of the Saints-Exposition of Chapters 8:17-39, Zondervan Publishing House, Fifth Printing, 1980.
Spiritual Depression It's Causes and Its Cure, Wm. B. Eerdmans Publishing Company, Reprinted March 1987.

Lockyer, Herbert, ***All the Men of The Bible,*** Zondervan Publishing House, Copyright 1958.
All The Kings and Queens of The Bible, Zondervan Publishing House, Copyright 1961.
All The Miracles of The Bible, Zondervan Publishing House, Copyright 1961.
All The Doctrines of The Bible, Zondervan Publishing House, Twenty-Second Printing 1982.

MacArthur, John Jr., ***Beware The Pretenders-Who are the Spiritual Masqueraders Jude Warns Against?,*** Victor Books, Copyright 1980.
Found: God's Will-God Wants to Give Your Life Direction and Purpose, Victor Books, Copyright 1973.
Our Sufficiency in Christ, John F. Macarthur Jr., copyright 1991.
The Charismatics-Doctrinal Perspective, John F. MacArthur Jr., Copyright 1987.
Condemned and Crucified-Matthew 27:11-56, Word of Grace Communications, Copyright 1987.
Lighting The Path-How To Study The Bible, Word of Grace Communications, Copyright 1982.

Acting on the Good News-Romans 1:1-16, Word of Grace Communications, Copyright 1987.

Body Dynamics-A Blueprint for the Church as a Body-A Fresh and Exciting View of What the Church Can Be, Victor Books, Second Printing, 1983.

God, Satan and Angels, Moody Press, 6th Printing, 1993.

Your Completeness in Christ-Colossians 1:24-2:23, Moody Press, Copyright 1985.

The Believer's Armor-Ephesians 6:10-24, Moody Press, Copyright 1985.

Priorities Of A Faithful Teacher-2 Timothy 4:1-8, Moody Press, Copyright 1991.

Church Leadership -1 Timothy 3: 1-13, John F. MacArthur Jr. copyright 1989.

Living For Christ In A Cynical World-1 Peter 2:11-20; 3:1-7, John F. MacArthur Jr. copyright 1989.

Unashamed-2 Timothy 1:1-18, Moody Press, Copyright 1990.

Without Excuse: Principles of God's Judgment-Romans 2:1-16, Moody Press, Copyright 1990.

To Live Is Christ-Philippians 1:12-26, Moody Press, Copyright 1990.

Triumph Over Death, Word of Grace Communications, 1982.

Introduction to Biblical Counseling, John F. MacArthur Jr., Copyright 1994.

Successful Christian Parenting, Word Publishing, 1999.

MacDonald, Charles R., *Administration of the Work of the Local Church,* Central Seminary Press, Copyright 1973.

Machen, J. Gresham, *The Origen of Paul's Religion,* Wm. B. Eerdmans Pub. Co., Reprinted August 1978.

Mack, Michael C., *The Synergy Church-A Strategy for Integrating Small Groups and Sunday School,* Baker Books, Copyright 1996.

Malphurs, Aubrey, *Ministry Nuts and Bolts: What They Don't Teach Pastors in Seminary,* Kregel, Copyright 1997.

Maring, Norman H. and Winthrop S. Hudson, *A Baptist Manual of Polity and Practice,* Revised Edition, Copyright 1991.

Marshall, Alfred, *The New International Version Interlinear Greek-English New Testament,* Zondervan Publishing House, 1976.

Matteson, Earle E., *The Job Complex,* River City Press, Copyright 2004. *The Biblical Plan for Power,* Matteson Ministries, Copyright 1989.

Maynard, Michael, *A History of The Debate over I John 5:7-8,* Comma Publications, Copyright 1995.

McCarrell, William, *The Great Shepherd in Psalm Twenty-Three,* Cicero Bible Press, 2017.

McClure, Alexander, *The Translators Revived,* Maranatha Bible Society, 2008.

McDowell, Josh, *Evidence that Demands a Verdict-Historical Evidences for the Christian Faith,* Campus Crusade for Christ, Inc., Copyright 1972. *More Evidence that Demands a Verdict,* Campus Crusade for Christ, Inc., Copyright 1975.
Answers To Tough Questions Skeptics Ask About The Christian Faith, Campus Crusade for Christ, Inc., Copyright 1980.

McGee, J. Vernon, *Volume IV-Matthew-Romans-Thru The Bible With J. Vernon McGee,* Thru The Bible Radio, 1994.

McLachlan, Douglas R., *Reclaiming Authentic Fundamentalism,* American Association of Christian Schools, 1993.

McLaughlin, Raymond W., *Communication For The Church,* Zondervan Publishing House, Copyright, 1968.

McLoughlin, William G., *Isaac Backus on Church, State, and Calvinism,* President and Fellows of Harvard Collage, Copyright 1968.

Miller, Allen O. and M. Eugene Osterhaven (Translators), *The Heidelberg Catechism,* United Church Press, 1962.

Moffatt, James, *The Expositor's Greek Testament, ed. by W. R. Nicoll, Vol. 5,* Wm. B. Eerdmans Publishing Co., November 1980 printing.

Moody, D.L., *Notes from My Bible,* Baker Book House Company, August 1979.

Moore, David L., *Galatians: Grace Alone,* Regular Baptist Press, Copyright 1979.

Morgan, Campbell, *The Acts Of The Apostles,* Fleming H. Revell Company, Copyright 1924.

Morris, Leon, *Tyndale New Testament Commentaries, ed. R.V.G. Tasker, Vol. 20,* Wm. B. Eerdmans Publishing Co., November 1980 printing.
Galatians-Paul's Charter of Christian Freedom, InterVarsity Press, Copyright 1996.

Muck, Kenneth A., *Life and Love-Ecclesiastes and Song of Solomon,* Regular Baptist Press, 1981.

Mullen, Mickey R., *The Way The Truth and The Life,* Micky Mullen, Copyright 2001.

Murphey, Cecil B., (Compiled by), *Dictionary of Biblical Literacy,* Oliver-Nelson Books, Copyright 1989.

Murry, Andrew., *Abide in Christ,* Miracle Press, 1997.

Nash, Ronald H., *Christian Faith and Historical Understanding,* Zondervan Publishing House, 1984.

Nee, Watchman, *A Balanced Christian Life,* Christian Fellowship Publishers, Copyright 1981.

Nettleton, David, *Meet the Minor Prophets-Adult Student Manual,* Regular Baptist Press, 1985.

Newell, William R., *The Book of Revelation,* Moody Press, 1978 printing.
Hebrews Verse By Verse, Moody Press, Reprinted 1978.
Romans Verse By Verse, Moody Press, Reprinted 1978.

Nicoll, W. Robertson (Editor), *The Expositor's Greek Testament, Volume One-The Gospel of St. John, Volume Two-Apostles, Romans & First Corinthians, Volume Three-Second Corinthians, Galatians, Ephesians, Philippians & Colossians, Volume Four-Thessalonians, Timothy, Titus, Philemon, Hebrews & James, Volume Five-First Peter, Second Peter, John, Jude & Revelation,* WM. B. Eerdmans Publishing Company, Reprinted November 1980.

The Sermon Outline Bible-Preacher's Homiletic Library-Colossians-James, Baker Book House, Reprinted 1979.

Noordtzij, A., ***The Bible Student's Commentary Numbers,*** Zondervan Publishing House, Copyright 1983.

North, Gary, ***Millennialism and Social Theory,*** Gary North, Copyright 1990.
Backward, Christian Soldiers, Institute for Christian Economics, Copyright 1984.

O'Brien, Peter T., ***44 Word Biblical Commentary-Colossians, Philemon,*** Word Incorporated, Copyright 1982.

Oehler, Gustave Friedrich, ***Theology of the Old Testament,*** Zondervan Publishing House, 2018.

Ogilvie, Lloyd J., ***The Communicator's Commentary-Acts,*** Word Book, Publisher, 1983.
The Communicator's Commentary-1,2 Thessalonians, 1,2 Timothy, Titus, Word Book Publisher, 1984.

Orthner, Donald, ***Wellsprings of Life-Understanding Proverbs,*** Adon Books, Third Printing, September1992.

Paige, Richard L. Jr., ***The Church Christ Built,*** North Star Baptist Press, Reprinted 1999.

Pelikan, Jaroslav and Walter A. Hansen, ***Luther's Works Volume 27 Lectures on Galatians,*** Concordia Publishing House, Copyright 1964.

Pfeiffer, Charles F. and Harrison, Everett F., ***The Wycliffe Bible Commentary,*** Moody Press Nineteenth Printing, 1981.

Phillips, John, ***Exploring Revelation,*** Loizeaux Brothers, 1991 Edition.
Exploring Acts, Loizeaux Brothers, 1991 Edition.
100 Sermon Outlines From The Old Testament, Moody Press, Second Printing, 1980.

Pickering, Ernest, ***Biblical Separation-The Struggle for a Pure Church,*** Regular Baptist Press, Fourth Printing, 1983.
The Theology of Evangelism, Regular Baptist Press, Copyright 1984.
The Tragedy of Compromise, Bob Jones University Press, Copyright 1994.

Phillips, John, *Exploring Revelation,* Loizeaux Brothers, 1991.

Pink, Arthur, W., *Exposition of the Gospel of John,* Zondervan Publishing House, Copyright 1975.
The Sovereignty of God, The Banner of Truth Trust, Reprinted 1972.
The Doctrine of Revelation, Baker Book House, Copyright 1975.
The Attributes of God, Baker Book House, Seventh Printing, 1980.

Ellingsen, Harald F.J. (Editor), *Preacher's Homiletic Library-Matthew-Volume 1,* Baker Book House, Reprinted 1979.
Preacher's Homiletic Library, Mark-Luke-Volume 2, Baker Book House, Reprinted 1979.
Preacher's Homiletic Library, John-Volume 3, Baker Book House, Reprinted 1979.
Preacher's Homiletic Library-Nicoll, Robertson W. (Editor), *Genesis-II Samuel-Volume 1,* Baker Book House, Reprinted 1979
Preacher's Homiletic Library-Nicoll, Robertson W. (Editor), *Psalm 77-Malachi-Volume 2,* Baker Book House, Reprinted 1979.
Preacher's Homiletic Library-Nicoll, Robertson W. (Editor), *Matthew 1-21-Volume 3,* Baker Book House, Reprinted 1979.
Preacher's Homiletic Library-Nicoll, Robertson W. (Editor), *Luke 1-John 3-Volume 4,* Baker Book House, Reprinted 1979.
Preacher's Homiletic Library-Nicoll, Robertson W. (Editor), *Acts 7-I Corinthians-Volume 5,* Baker Book House, Reprinted 1979.
Preacher's Homiletic Library-Turnbull, Ralph G. (Editor), *Matthew to Luke-Volume 1,* Baker Book House, Reprinted 1979.
Preacher's Homiletic Library – Turnbull, Ralph G. (Editor), *I Corinthians to Colossians-Volume 3,* Baker Book House, Reprinted 1979.
Preacher's Homiletic Library – Turnbull, Ralph G. (Editor), *First Thessalonians to Hebrews-Volume 4,* Baker Book House, Reprinted 1979.

Piper, John, *The Passion of Jesus Christ,* Crossway Books, Copyright 2004.

Radmacher, Earl D., *What the Church Is All About,* Moody Press, 1978 Edition.

Ramm, Bernard L., *Hermeneutics,* Baker Book House, 1987.

Ravenhill, Leonard, *A Classic on Revival-Why Revival Tarries,* Bethany House Publishers, 1983.

Reid, Daniel G., Robert D. Linder, Bruce L. Shelley, Harry S. Stout (Editor), *Dictionary of Christianity in America,* InterVarsity Press, 1990.

Rice, John R., *I Am a Fundamentalist,* Sword of the Lord Publishers, 1975.
God's Work-How to Do It, Sword of the Lord Publishers, 1971.
The Golden Path To Successful Personal Soul Winning, Sword of the Lord Publishers, Copyright 1961.
Predestined for Hell? NO!, Sword of the Lord Publishers, 1953.
You Must Be Born Again, Sword of the Lord Publishers, 1953.
When Skeletons Come out of their Closets!, Sword of the Lord Publishers, Fifth Printing July 1971.
The Rice Reference Bible, Thomas Nelson, Inc., Copyright 1981.

Richards, Lawrence O., *Expository Dictionary of Bible Worlds,* Zondervan Publishing House, 1985.

Ridderbos, J., *Bible Student's Commentary Deuteronomy,* Zondervan Publishing House, 1984.
Bible Student's Commentary Isaiah, Zondervan Publishing House, 1985.

Rimmer, Harry, *The Last of The Giants,* Reprinted by Christian Book Gallery, 1948.

Robertson, Archibald T., *Word Pictures In The New Testament, Matthew Mark- Volume I,* Baker Book House, 1930.
Luke- Volume II, Baker Book House, 1930.
Acts- Volume III, Baker Book House, 1930.
Epistles of Paul- Volume IV, Baker Book House, 1931.
John Hebrews- Volume V, Baker Book House, 1932.
Volume VI, Baker Book House, 1933.

Robinson, Haddon W., *Biblical Preaching-The Development and Delivery of Expository Messages,* Baker Book House, Fourth Printing, 1981.

Rodgers, Thomas R., *The Panorama of The Old Testament,* Impact Press, Third Printing, 1991.
Strategy-A Sourcebook of Tactics For A Dynamic Ministry, Impact Press, Copyright, 1983.

Russell, D.S., *Between the Testaments,* Fortress Press, Sixth Printing, 1979.

Ryrie, Charles Caldwell, *Revelation,* Moody Press, Seventeenth Printing, 1979.
The Holy Spirit, Moody Press, Ninth Printing, 1973.
Basic Theology, Victor Books, 1999.

Saucy, Robert L., *The Church in God's Program,* Moody Press, Published 1972.

Saxe, Raymond H., *The Battle for Your Bible,* Grace Bible Publications, Second Printing 1978.

Schaeffer, Francis A., *The God Who Is There,* Inter-Varsity Press, Copyright, 1968.
He Is There and He Is not Silent, Tyndale House Publishers, Fifteenth Printing, 1981.
How Should We Then Live?-The Rise and Decline of Western Thought and Culture, Crossway Books, Copyright July 1976.

Schaff, Philip, *History of the Christian Church-Apostolic Christianity-Volume I,* W.M. B. Eerdmans Publishing Company, Reprinted July 1980.
History of the Christian Church-Ante-Nicene Christianity-Volume II, WM. B. Eerdmans Publishing Company, Tenth Printing, July 1980.
History of the Christian Church-Nicene and Ante-nicene Christianity-Volume III, WM. B. Eerdmans Publishing Company, Reprinted April 1979.
History of the Christian Church-Mediaeval Christianity-Volume IV, WM. B. Eerdmans Publishing Company, Reprinted April 1979.
History of the Christian Church-The Middle Ages-Volume V, WM. B. Eerdmans Publishing Company, Reprinted April 1979.
History of the Christian Church-The Middle Ages-Volume VI, WM. B. Eerdmans Publishing Company, Reprinted July 1980.
History of the Christian Church-Modern Christianity-Volume VII, WM. B. Eerdmans Publishing Company, Reprinted April 1979.
History of the Christian Church-Modern Christianity-Volume VIII, WM. B. Eerdmans Publishing Company, Reprinted April 1979.
A Christian Manifesto, Crossway Books, Copyright 1982.

Schein, Bruce E., *Following The Way-The Setting of John's Gospel,* Augsburg Publishing House, Copyright 1980.

Shedd, William G.T., *Shedd's Dogmatic Theology-Volume I, Shedd's Dogmatic Theology-Volume II, Shedd's Dogmatic Theology-Volume III,* Tomas Nelson Publishers, Second Edition, 1980.

Sheldon, Charles M., *In His Steps-What Would Jesus Do?,* Grosset & Dunlap, 1935.

Soltau, Henry W., *The Holy Vessels and Furniture of the Tabernacle,* Kregal Publications, Reprinted 1975.
The Tabernacle, the Priesthood and the Offerings, Kregal Publications, Second Printing, 1974.

Sproul, R.C., *Faith Alone The Evangelical Doctrine of Justification,* Baker Books Second Printing, 1996.

Spurgeon, Charles H., *The Parables of Our Lord,* Baker Book House, Six Volumes, Reprinted 1979.

Spurgeon, Charles H., *The Treasury of David,* Baker Book House, Seven Volumes, Second Printing July 1978.

Spurgeon, Charles H., *12 Sermons on Backsliding,* Baker Book House, Reprinted 1979.
The Passion and Death of Christ, William B. Eerdmans Publishing Company, Reprinted October 1979.

Stott, John R.W., *The Message of Ephesians,* Inter-Varsity Press, 1984.

Strauch, Alexander, *Biblical Eldership-An Urgent Call To Restore Biblical Church Leadership,* Lewis and Roth Publishers, Copyright 1995.

Stravinskas, Peter M.J. (Editor), *Our Sunday Visitor's Catholic Encyclopedia,* Our Sunday Visitor Publishing Division, Copyright 1991.

Streeter, Lloyd L., *Seventy-five Problems,* Lloyd L. Streeter, Copyright 2001.

Sturz, Harry A., *The Byzantine Text-Type & New Testament Textual Criticism,* Biblical Viewpoints Publications, Copyright 1984.

Tasker, R.V.G General Editor, Tyndale New Testament Commentaries, Twenty Volumes, Wm. B. Eerdmans Publishing Company, Eighth Printing, July 1980

Teachout, Raymond L., *Breaking Down the Walls...and the Gospel,* EBPA Publications Second Printing, 1999.

Tenney, Merrill C. and Steven Barabas, *The Zondervan Pictorial Encyclopedia of the Bible, Volumes One through Five,* Zondervan Publishing House, 2009.

Thomas, David, *Acts of the Apostles-Expository and Homiletical,* Kregel Publications, Published 1980.
Gospel of John- Expository and Homiletical, Kregel Publications, Published 1980.

Thomas, Major W. Ian, *The Saving Life of Christ,* Daybreak Books, Published 1961.

Torrey, R.A. -Editor and Others, Five Volumes, Baker Book House, Reprinted 1980.

Tillapaugh, Frank R., *Unleashing the Church-Getting People Out of the Fortress and Into Ministry,* Regal Books, Copyright 1982.

Torrey R.A. and Charles Leach, *Our Bible-How We Got It and Ten Reasons Why I Believe the Bible is the Word of God,* Fleming H. Revell Company, Copyright 1898.

Unger, Merrill F., *The Baptizing Work of The Holy Spirit,* Van Kampen Press Inc., Copyright 1953.
The Baptism & Gifts of The Holy Spirit, Moody Press, Copyright 1974.
The New Unger's Bible Dictionary, Moody Press, Copyright 1988.
Unger's Survey of the Bible, Harvest House Publishers, Reprinted 1981, 3rd printing, March 1985.
Zechariah: Prophet of Messiah's Glory, Zondervan Publishing House, Twelfth Printing, 1982.
Volume II Unger's Commentary on the Old Testament, Moody Press, 1981.

Van Doren, W.H., *Gospel of John,* Kregel Publications, Copyright 1981.

Van Gorder, Paul R., *The Church Stands Corrected,* Victor Books, Copyright 1967.

Vincent, Marvin R., *Word Studies in the New Testament,* **Three Volumes,** Wm. B. Eerdmans's Publishing Co., Seventh Printing, 1980.

Vincent, Milton R., *Word Studies in The New Testament-Volume IV,* WM. B. Eerdmans Publishing Co., Seventh Reprinting, 1980.

Walton, Arthur B., *The Heartbeat of Paul-The Book of 2 Corinthians,* Regular Baptist Press, Copyright 1978.
Marks of A Mighty Church-First and Second Thessalonians, Regular Baptist Press, Copyright 1982.

Walvoord, John F., *The Rapture Question,* The Zondervan Corporation, Second Printing, 1976.

Walvoord, John F. and John E. Walvoord, *The Rapture Question, Revised and Enlarge Edition,* The Zondervan Corporation, Seventheeth Printing, 1980.
The Holy Spirit At Work Today, Moody Press, Second Printing, 1973.
Daniel The Key To Prophetic Revelation, Moody Paperback Edition, 1989.

Warfield, Benjamin Breckinridge, *The Inspiration and Authority of the Bible,* The Presbyterian and Reformed Publishing Company, Sixth Printing, 1970.
Revelation and Inspiration-Volume I, Baker Book House, reprinted 1981.
Biblical Doctrines-Volume II, Baker Book House, Reprinted 1981.
Christology and Criticism-Volume III, Baker Book House, Reprinted 1981.
Studies in Tertullian and Augustine-Volume IV, Baker Book House, Reprinted 1981.
Calvin and Calvinism-Volume V, Baker Book House, reprinted 1981.
The Westminster Assembly and Its Work-Volume VI, Baker Book House, Reprinted 1981.
Perfectionism Part one-Volume VII, Baker Book House, Reprinted 1981.
Perfectionism Part two-Volume VIII, Baker Book House, Reprinted 1981.
Studies in Theology-Volume IX, Baker Book House, Reprinted 1981.
Critical Reviews-Volume X, Baker Book House, Reprinted 1981.

Weisiger, Cary N. III, *Preacher's Homiletic Library-Proclaiming the New Testament, 1st Peter to Revelation Vol. 5,* Baker Book House, Copyright 1961.

Weiss, Christian G., *Insights Into Bible Times and Customs,* Back to the Bible Publication, Copyright 1972.

Welch, Wilbert W., *Conduct Becoming Saints-The Book of 1 Corinthians Part 2, Chapters 9-16,* Regular Baptist Press, Copyright 1978.
A Charge to Keep-The Book of First Timothy, Regular Baptist Press, Copyright 1982.

Wesley, John, *Sermons-Volume II,* Eaton & Mains, 1985.

Whitcomb, John C., *Everyman's Bible Commentary-Daniel,* Moody Press, 1985.
Everyman's Bible Commentary-Esther, Moody Press, 1979.

Whitcomb, John C. and Donald B. Deyoung, *The Moon-It's Creation, Form and Significance,* John the Baptist Printing Ministry, 1978.

White, John, *Arise and Build! Ezra and Nehemiah,* Regular Baptist Press, 1979.
Song of the Saints-A Study of Selected Psalms, Regular Baptist Press, 1980.

Wiersbe, Warren W., *Be Faithful-1-2 Timothy, Titus, Philemon,* Victor Books, 1981.
Walking with The Giants-A Minister's Guide to Good Reading and Great Preaching, Baker Book House, Copyright 1976.
Listening to The Giants, Baker Book House, Copyright 1980.

Williamson, G.A. (Translator), *The History of The Church-Eusebius,* Dorset Press, 1984.

Winter, Ernst F. (Translator and Editor), *Erasmus-Luther Discourse on Free Will,* The Continuum Publishing Company, Copyright 1961.

Wood, Leon J., *Downfall and Deliverance-The Book of Judges,* Regular Baptist Press, Copyright 1975.

Wood, Leon J., Revised by David O'Brien, *A Survey of Israel's History,* Zondervan Corporation, Copyright 1986.

Wuest, Kenneth S., *The New Testament-An Expanded Translation,* Wm. B. Eerdmans Publishing Company, Three Volumes, Twelfth Printing, July 1980.
Philippians, In the Greek New Testament for The English Reader, Wm. B. Eerdmans Publishing Company, Copyright 1942.

Young, Edward J. Young, *The Book of Isaiah, Three Volumes,* Wm. B. Eerdman's Publishing Co., Reprinted November 1992.

Zodhihiates, Spiros, *The Behavior of Belief,* Wm. B. Eerdman's Publishing Co., fourth printing, 1973.
The Church in Prophecy, Zondervan Publishing House, 16th Printing, 1980.

www.ingramcontent.com/pod-product-compliance
Lightning Source LLC
Chambersburg PA
CBHW071312150726
47997CB00002B/453